Essex Works.
For a better quality of life

WAB

D0589751

Kitc
favourites

MARY BERRY'S
Kitchen favourites

Informal everyday recipes for family and friends

LONDON, NEW YORK, MELBOURNE,
MUNICH AND DELHI

Editor ELIZABETH WATSON
Senior art editor HELEN SPENCER
Executive managing editor ADÈLE HAYWARD
Managing art editor NICK HARRIS
DTP designer TRACI SALTER
Senior jacket creative NICOLA POWLING
Production controller MANDY INNESS
Art director PETER LUFF
Publisher MARY-CLARE JERRAM

Photography DAVE KING

DORLING KINDERSLEY (INDIA)
Editor PANKHOORI SINHA
Senior editor DIPALI SINGH
Designer ENOSH FRANCIS
Senior designer KAVITA DUTTA
DTP designer HARISH AGGARWAL, TARUN SHARMA
DTP co-ordinator PANKAJ SHARMA
Head of publishing APARNA SHARMA

Material first published in *Mary Berry's Complete Cookbook* in 1995
This paperback edition published in Great Britain in 2011
by Dorling Kindersley Limited
80 Strand, London, WC2R 0RL

A Penguin Company

2 4 6 8 10 9 7 5 3 1

001–MD389–Jul/11

A CIP catalogue record for this books is available
from the British Library.

ISBN 978-1-4053-7351-7

Printed in
China by Leo

See our complete catalogue at
www.dk.com

CONTENTS

INTRODUCTION

Home cooking, for me, is all about sharing my love of food with family and friends. However, people are finding it harder to fit a nutritious home-cooked meal into their busy lives.

These recipes, I hope, will inspire you to cook some of my favourite recipes. From light suppers to hearty family meals, and from recipes that cater for more adventurous tastes, to traditional rustic dishes, there will be something for everyone in this special collection of my kitchen favourites.

I start with a selection of tasty soups and starters that are foolproof ways to start off any meal: French Onion Soup and Swiss Double-Cheese Soufflés are all quicker to make than you'd think. Soup is economical too – try doubling the batch you make and take it to work in a flask for a cheap and nutritious lunch.

My recipes are foolproof and build your confidence as a home cook, so you can't go wrong with the next chapter on fish and seafood. Keep it simple with Crispy-topped Seafood Pie or impress your guests with Lobster Tails with Mango & Lime.

When it comes to preparing quick evening meals my poultry and meat chapter is full of delicious recipes, with new and exotic dishes from around the world, as well as those old favourites such as Beef Bourguignon and Lancashire Hot Pot.

Next comes an essential vegetarian chapter. Vegetarian food can so often be dull and predictable, so I've carefully chosen a variety of imaginative and nutritious dishes to

cater for the strictest of diets. The Vegetarian Bakes and Casseroles are great if you are entertaining as they are perfect for the vegetarian main course, but the meat eaters will also enjoy a spoonful or two alongside their own main course. Indian and oriental cuisine, with its aromatic and pungent spices, lends itself particularly well to vegetables. Try serving a selection of these dishes alongside rice and breads.

When it comes to fast food, you can't get quicker than pasta and rice. I've dedicated a chapter to my favourite pasta and rice dishes – natural convenience foods that are quick to prepare and incredibly versatile. For a simple supper, rustle up Tuna and Fennel Pasta Bake or Risotto al Verde.

In the vegetable and salads chapter you will find a collection of appetizing dishes that you can put together with minimum fuss and time. Summer Peas & Beans will top up your five-a-day, and a moreish Gratin Dauphinois is the perfect accompaniment to classic roasts, or you could try serving it as a main dish with salad, for a light supper.

Last, but not least, I've dedicated a good few pages to my favourite hot and cold puddings, which I hope will inspire budding cooks to dust off their mixing bowls and have a go. From Lemon Syllabub to Apple Strudel, all my desserts are designed to be easy to prepare, quick, and above all, tasty.

Short on time, but big on taste, I hope my collection of kitchen favourites will become yours too.

Soups & Starters

THAI SPICED SOUP

SERVES 4

90g (3oz) thin egg noodles
salt and black pepper
500ml (16fl oz) chicken stock
1 x 400g (13oz) can coconut milk
1 small carrot, coarsely chopped
30g (1oz) French beans, cut into
   1 cm (½in) pieces
3 spring onions, thinly sliced
250g (8oz) cooked lean boneless
   and skinless chicken, shredded
125g (4oz) mixed green leaves, such
   as spinach and pak choi, shredded
30g (1oz) bean sprouts
1tbsp fish sauce
2tsp Thai curry paste (green or red)
¼ cucumber, cut into matchstick-
   thin strips, and coriander sprigs
   to garnish

1 Cook the noodles in boiling salted water for 2–3 minutes, or according to package instructions, until just tender. Drain and rinse in cold water. Set aside while preparing the soup.

2 Put the stock, coconut milk, carrot, French beans, and spring onions into a large saucepan, and bring to a boil.

3 Lower the heat, add the chicken, green leaves, bean sprouts, fish sauce, and spice paste, and cook for 2 minutes or until the green leaves are just wilted. Season to taste with salt and pepper.

4 To serve, divide the cooked noodles among warmed bowls. Ladle the hot soup over the noodles, and garnish with cucumber strips and coriander sprigs.

Cook's know-how

For a vegetarian version, omit the cooked chicken and use a vegetable stock instead of the chicken stock. You can also vary the vegetables, but their cooking times may be different. Try shredded white cabbage instead of the green leaves and mangetout instead of French beans. Shredded Swiss chard would also be good in this soup, as would a small quantity of sweetcorn kernels or peas, and even a little diced aubergine.

FRENCH ONION SOUP

SERVES 8

45g (1½oz) butter
1tbsp sunflower oil
1kg (2lb) large onions, thinly sliced
2tsp caster sugar
30g (1oz) plain flour
1.8 litres (3 pints) vegetable, chicken, or beef stock
salt and black pepper
8 Gruyère croûtes (see box, below)

1 Melt the butter with the oil in a large saucepan, and caramelize the onions with the sugar (see box, below). Sprinkle the flour into the pan and cook, stirring constantly, for 1–2 minutes.

2 Gradually stir in the stock and bring to a boil. Season with salt and pepper, then cover and simmer, stirring from time to time, for 35 minutes.

3 Taste the soup for seasoning, then ladle into warmed bowls. Float a Gruyère croûte in each bowl and serve at once.

Cook's know-how

Cooking with sugar is the key to developing a rich, golden brown colour and sweet caramel flavour in onions. It is this that produces the characteristic appearance and taste of this classic soup.

CARAMELIZING ONIONS

Cook the onions in the butter and oil for a few minutes until soft. Add the sugar and continue cooking over a low heat, stirring occasionally, for 20 minutes or until the onions are golden brown.

GRUYERE CROUTES

Cut slices from a baguette and toast on one side under a hot grill. Remove from the heat and turn the slices over. Grate Gruyère cheese evenly over the untoasted sides of the bread slices. Return to the grill and cook until the cheese has melted and is gently bubbling.

CREAMY CARROT & ORANGE SOUP

SERVES 6–8

30g (1oz) butter
1 onion, coarsely chopped
1kg (2lb) carrots, thickly sliced
1.5 litres (2½ pints) vegetable
  or chicken stock
grated zest of ½ orange
1 x 200ml carton orange juice
salt and black pepper
1 x 200ml carton crème fraîche
3tbsp snipped fresh chives

1 Melt the butter in a large saucepan, add the onion, and cook gently, stirring occasionally, for a few minutes until soft but not coloured. Add the carrots, cover, and cook gently, stirring from time to time, for 10 minutes.

2 Add the stock and bring to a boil. Cover and simmer, stirring from time to time, for 30–40 minutes until the carrots are soft.

3 Purée the soup in a food processor or blender until smooth. Return the soup to the rinsed-out pan, add the orange zest and juice, and salt and pepper to taste. Stir in the crème fraîche and then gently reheat the soup.

4 Stir in half of the snipped chives, and garnish individual servings with the remaining chives.

Healthy option

The crème fraîche makes this soup rich and creamy for a dinner party first course, but for an everyday soup that is full of zest and vitality, you can easily omit it and increase the stock by 1 x 200ml carton in step 2. Another healthy option is to cook the onion in step 1 in 1tbsp each olive oil and water rather than using butter.

SERVES 8

600ml (1 pint) milk
2 bay leaves
¼tsp grated nutmeg
90g (3oz) butter
2 large onions, finely sliced
75g (2½oz) plain flour
1.5 litres (2½ pints) vegetable or
  chicken stock
salt and black pepper
150g (5oz) blue Stilton cheese,
  grated
single cream to serve
  (optional)

BLUE STILTON & ONION SOUP

1 Pour the milk into a saucepan, add the bay leaves and nutmeg, and bring almost to a boil. Remove from the heat, cover, and leave to infuse for 20 minutes.

2 Meanwhile, melt the butter in a large pan, add the onions, and cook very gently, stirring occasionally, for about 10 minutes or until they are soft but not coloured.

3 Add the flour, and cook, stirring, for 2 minutes. Strain the milk and gradually blend it into the onion and flour. Add the stock, and season with salt and pepper. Bring to a boil and simmer, half covered, for 10 minutes.

4 Add the cheese and stir over a very low heat until it melts (do not boil or the cheese will be stringy). Taste for seasoning, and stir in a little cream if you wish. Serve hot.

Healthy option

There are ways of making this soup lighter if you are concerned about the fat content. Use semi-skimmed milk in step 1, only 30g (1oz) butter in step 2, and omit the flour in step 3. At the end, whisk the flour to a paste with a little cold stock or water, then whisk into the soup and boil, whisking, until thickened. Add only 60–90g (2–3oz) cheese in step 4.

CHINESE CRAB & SWEETCORN SOUP

SERVES 4

375g (12oz) frozen sweetcorn kernels
1 litre (1¾ pints) hot chicken stock
3 spring onions, thinly sliced
1cm (½in) piece of fresh root ginger,
  peeled and grated
1 garlic clove, crushed
1tbsp light soy sauce
250g (8oz) cooked white crabmeat
1tbsp cornflour mixed with 2tbsp
  cold water
salt and black pepper
sesame oil and coriander sprigs
  to serve

1 Purée the sweetcorn with one-quarter of the hot stock in a food processor or blender until smooth.

2 Pour the remaining stock into a pan, and add the spring onions, ginger, garlic, and soy sauce. Heat until bubbles form at the edge.

3 Add the crabmeat and the sweetcorn purée, and continue to heat until bubbles form again. Blend the cornflour mixture into the soup, and cook, stirring occasionally, for 10 minutes or until it thickens slightly. Season to taste with salt and pepper.

4 Pour the soup into bowls, drizzle a little sesame oil over each serving, and garnish with coriander. Serve hot.

SERVES 4

175g (6oz) white cabbage, coarsely
  shredded
200g (7oz) waxy potatoes, diced
1 x 225g (8oz) can chopped tomatoes
1 small carrot, chopped
1 small onion, chopped
1.5 litres (2½ pints) vegetable or chicken
  stock, more if needed
500g (1lb) cooked beetroot, peeled
  and diced
3–4 dill sprigs, chopped
30g (1oz) sugar
2tbsp wine vinegar
salt and black pepper
soured cream and dill sprigs
  to garnish

BORSCHT

1 Put the cabbage, potatoes, tomatoes, carrot, and onion into a large pan with the stock.

2 Bring to a boil, then simmer for 30–40 minutes until the vegetables are very tender. Add extra stock if necessary.

3 Add the diced beetroot, dill, sugar, and vinegar, and simmer for 10 minutes to let the sweet-sour flavours develop. Add salt and pepper to taste, and more sugar and vinegar if necessary.

4 Serve at once, garnished with spoonfuls of soured cream and sprigs of dill.

SOMERSET MUSHROOM SOUP

SERVES 4–6

30g (1oz) butter
1 small onion, finely chopped
1 garlic clove, crushed
500g (1lb) mushrooms, sliced
1.25 litres (2 pints) vegetable or
  chicken stock
150ml (¼ pint) dry white wine
2tsp chopped fresh marjoram
2tbsp chopped fresh thyme
salt and black pepper

1 Melt the butter in a large saucepan, add the onion and garlic, and cook gently, stirring occasionally, for a few minutes until soft but not coloured. Add the mushrooms and cook, stirring from time to time, for 10 minutes.

2 Pour in the stock and wine, then add the marjoram and half of the thyme, and season with salt and pepper. Bring to a boil, cover, and simmer gently for 10 minutes or until the mushrooms are tender.

3 Taste for seasoning and serve hot, sprinkled with the remaining fresh thyme.

CURRIED PARSNIP SOUP

SERVES 6–8

30g (1oz) butter
750g (1½lb) parsnips, coarsely
  chopped
1 large onion, chopped
1 large garlic clove, crushed
2tsp mild curry powder
1.8 litres (3 pints) vegetable or
  chicken stock
salt and black pepper
200ml (7fl oz) single cream
fresh chives to garnish

1 Melt the butter in a large saucepan, add the chopped parsnips, onion, and crushed garlic, and cook gently, stirring occasionally, for 5 minutes or until the onion is softened but not coloured.

2 Stir in the curry powder, and cook for 1 minute, then blend in the stock, and season with salt and pepper. Bring to a boil, stirring, then cover, and simmer gently for 20 minutes or until the parsnips are tender.

3 Purée the soup in a food processor or blender until smooth. Return the soup to the rinsed-out pan, heat gently to warm through, stirring constantly, then taste for seasoning.

4 Stir in the single cream and reheat gently. Serve at once, garnished with fresh chives.

Healthy option

If you are concerned about the fat content, omit the cream and use stock or water instead.

WINTER VEGETABLE SOUP

SERVES 6

45g (1½oz) butter
1 leek, trimmed and diced
1 onion, chopped
1 celery stalk, diced
1 small potato, diced
1 turnip, diced
1 small carrot, diced
3 garlic cloves, crushed
1.5 litres (2½ pints) vegetable or
  chicken stock
250g (8oz) spinach, coarsely shredded
  (see box, below)
3 spring onions, thinly sliced
salt and black pepper

1 Melt the butter in a large saucepan, add the leek, and cook gently, stirring occasionally, for 5 minutes or until softened. Add the onion, celery, potato, turnip, carrot, and garlic, and cook for 8 minutes.

2 Pour in the stock, and bring to a boil. Cover and simmer, stirring occasionally, for 25 minutes or until the vegetables are tender.

3 Add the spinach and spring onions, and cook for just 3 minutes until the spinach is wilted and still bright green. Season well, and serve hot.

SHREDDING SPINACH

Remove the stalks and stack several spinach leaves. Roll up tightly, and cut crosswise into shreds.

VEGETABLE MINESTRONE

SERVES 4–6

2 tbsp olive oil
1 onion, chopped
2 celery stalks, chopped
2 carrots, diced
1 x 400g (14oz) can chopped
  Italian plum tomatoes
1 tbsp tomato purée
1 garlic clove, crushed
salt and black pepper
1.5 litres (2½ pints) chicken or
  vegetable stock
1 x 400g (14oz) can cannellini or
  red kidney beans, drained
250g (8oz) leeks, trimmed and
  finely sliced
125g (4oz) Savoy cabbage,
  finely shredded
2 tbsp arborio (risotto) rice
grated Parmesan cheese to serve

1 Heat the oil in a large saucepan, add the onion, celery, and carrots, and cook gently, stirring, for 5 minutes.

2 Add the tomatoes, tomato purée, and garlic, and season with salt and pepper. Stir, then pour in the stock and bring to a boil over a high heat.

3 Cover the pan and lower the heat so the soup is a gently simmering. Cook for 15 minutes, stirring occasionally.

4 Add the beans, leeks, cabbage, and rice, and simmer for a further 20 minutes. Taste for seasoning.

5 Serve hot, with a bowl of grated Parmesan cheese for everyone to help themselves.

Cook's know-how

If you haven't got arborio or any other type of risotto rice, use broken spaghetti instead. You will need 30g (1oz).

GAZPACHO

SERVES 4–6

1kg (2lb) tomatoes, peeled (see box, below), quartered, and seeded
1 large Spanish onion
1 x 200g (7oz) jar roasted peppers (in oil or brine), drained
2 large garlic cloves
600ml (1 pint) cold vegetable or chicken stock
75ml (2½fl oz) olive oil
4tbsp red wine vinegar
juice of ½ lemon
salt and black pepper

TO GARNISH

½ cucumber, diced
1 small green pepper, halved, seeded, and diced
garlic croûtons (see box, below)

1 Coarsely chop the tomatoes, onion, peppers, and garlic. Purée in a food processor or blender with the stock, oil, and vinegar until smooth.

2 Turn the mixture into a bowl and add the lemon juice, and salt and pepper to taste. Cover and chill for at least 1 hour.

3 Serve the soup well chilled in bowls, each one garnished with spoonfuls of diced cucumber, green pepper, and garlic croûtons.

PEELING TOMATOES

Cut the cores from the tomatoes and score an "x" on the base. Immerse the tomatoes in boiling water for 8–15 seconds until their skins start to split. Transfer at once to cold water. When the tomatoes are cool enough to handle, peel off the skin with a small knife.

GARLIC CROUTONS

Trim the crusts from slices of bread and cut into 1cm (½in) cubes. Heat a very thin film of oil in a non-stick frying pan. Peel and crush 1 garlic clove and cook for 1 minute. Add the bread cubes and cook, stirring occasionally, until brown all over. Remove, and drain on paper towels.

CHILLED CURRIED APPLE & MINT SOUP

SERVES 6

30g (1oz) butter
1 onion, coarsely chopped
1tbsp mild curry powder
900ml (1½ pints) vegetable stock
750g (1½lb) cooking apples, peeled, cored, and coarsely chopped
2tbsp mango chutney
juice of ½ lemon
7–8 sprigs of fresh mint
salt and black pepper
100g (3½oz) plain yogurt
a little milk, if needed

1 Melt the butter in a large saucepan, add the onion, and cook gently, stirring occasionally, for a few minutes until soft but not coloured. Add the curry powder and cook, stirring constantly, for 1–2 minutes.

2 Add the stock and chopped apples and bring to a boil, stirring. Cover and simmer for 15 minutes or until the apples are tender.

3 Purée the apple mixture, mango chutney, and lemon juice in a food processor or blender until very smooth.

4 Strip the mint leaves from the stalks, reserving 6 small sprigs for garnish. Finely chop the mint leaves.

5 Pour the soup into a large bowl, stir in the chopped mint, and add salt and pepper to taste. Cover and chill in the refrigerator for at least 3 hours.

6 Whisk in the yogurt, then taste for seasoning. If the soup is too thick, add a little milk. Garnish with the reserved mint before serving.

Cook's know-how

This soup is equally delicious served hot. After puréeing, return soup to the rinsed-out pan and reheat it gently, stirring it occasionally. Stir in the chopped mint, then remove from the heat and swirl in the yoghurt. Serve at once.

CHEVRE CROUTES

SERVES 4

½ long, slim baguette
about 2tbsp ready-made pesto
1 log-shaped goat's cheese
olive oil for sprinkling
black pepper
radicchio and frisée leaves to serve
chervil sprigs to garnish

1 Cut the baguette into 8 slices, 1cm (½in) thick, and toast under a hot grill on one side only. Lightly spread the untoasted sides of the baguette slices with the ready-made pesto.

2 Cut the goat's cheese into 8 slices, 1cm (½in) thick, and arrange on top of the pesto. Toast the topped croûtes under the hot grill, 7cm (3in) from the heat, for 3 minutes or until the cheese just begins to soften. Remove the grill pan from the heat.

3 Lightly sprinkle a little olive oil and grind a little pepper over each cheese croûte. Return the croûtes to the hot grill, close to the heat, for 3 minutes or until the cheese begins to bubble and is just tinged golden brown.

4 Line a serving platter with radicchio and frisée leaves, arrange the croûtes on top, and garnish with chervil sprigs. Serve at once.

Italian bruschetta with goat's cheese

Substitute 8 slices of Italian ciabatta for the baguette. After toasting the topped croûtes in step 3, sprinkle chopped pitted black olives over them and drizzle with extra virgin oilve oil. Serve sprinkled with fresh basil leaves.

WARM SALAD WITH BACON & SCALLOPS

SERVES 4

375g (12oz) mixed salad leaves, such as radicchio, lamb's lettuce, frisée, and rocket
8 shallots, finely chopped
1tbsp sunflower oil
250g (8oz) lean unsmoked bacon rashers, rinds removed, diced
12 scallops, halved
3tbsp white wine vinegar
2tbsp walnut oil
salt and black pepper

1 Put the salad leaves into a large bowl and sprinkle with half of the shallots.

2 Heat the oil in a frying pan, add the bacon, and cook quickly, stirring occasionally, for 5 minutes or until crisp. Add the scallops and cook quickly for 1–2 minutes until just opaque. Remove from the pan and keep warm.

3 Add the remaining shallots and cook for 1 minute. Add the vinegar and boil rapidly, stirring to incorporate the pan juices.

4 Sprinkle the walnut oil over the salad leaves and toss together until the leaves are evenly coated and shiny. Add the bacon and scallops, hot vinegar and shallots, and season to taste.

Cook's know-how

Stirring vinegar into the frying pan loosens and dissolves the flavoursome juices on the bottom of the pan so they are not wasted. This is called deglazing.

PRAWN COCKTAIL

SERVES 4

150ml (¼ pint) mayonnaise
2tbsp creamed horseradish
1tbsp lemon juice
1tsp Worcestershire sauce
1tsp tomato purée
¼tsp caster sugar
few drops of Tabasco sauce
black pepper
250g (8oz) shelled, cooked cold-water
    prawns
salad leaves to serve
thin lemon wedges, parsley sprigs, and
    4 large cooked prawns in their shells
    to garnish

1 Make the dressing: in a medium bowl, combine the mayonnaise, creamed horseradish, lemon juice, Worcestershire sauce, tomato purée, caster sugar, and Tabasco sauce, and season well with a little black pepper.

2 Add the peeled cooked prawns and stir to coat with the dressing.

3 Line 4 individual glass serving bowls with the salad leaves and top with the prawn mixture. Garnish each serving with a thin lemon wedge, a parsley sprig, and a large prawn.

SWISS DOUBLE CHEESE SOUFFLES

SERVES 6

45g (1½oz) butter, plus extra for
 greasing
45g (1½oz) plain flour
300ml (½ pint) milk
60g (2oz) Gruyère cheese, grated
2tbsp snipped fresh chives
salt and black pepper
3 eggs, separated
60g (2oz) Parmesan cheese, grated
300ml (½ pint) double cream
snipped fresh chives to garnish

1 Melt the butter in a large saucepan, add the flour, and cook, stirring, for 1 minute. Remove from the heat and gradually blend in the milk. Return to the heat and bring to a boil, stirring until the mixture thickens.

2 Remove the pan from the heat and beat in the Gruyère cheese and chives. Season with salt and pepper, and stir in the egg yolks. Whisk the egg whites until stiff but not dry. Stir 1tbsp into the mixture, then fold in the rest.

3 Generously butter 6 small ramekins, and divide the mixture equally among them. Place the ramekins in a small roasting tin, and pour boiling water into the tin to come halfway up the sides of the ramekins.

4 Bake the soufflés in a preheated oven at 220°C (425°F, Gas 7) for 15–20 minutes until golden and springy to the touch. Leave the soufflés to stand for 5–10 minutes; they will shrink by about one-third.

5 Butter a large shallow gratin dish. Sprinkle half of the Parmesan cheese over the bottom. Run a palette knife around the edge of each soufflé, unmould carefully, and arrange on top of the Parmesan in the gratin dish.

6 Season the cream with salt and pepper, and pour over the soufflés. Sprinkle the remaining Parmesan over the top, and return to the oven for 15–20 minutes until golden. Garnish with snipped chives.

ASPARAGUS WITH QUICK HOLLANDAISE

SERVES 4

625g (1¼lb) asparagus
salt and black pepper
lemon twists to garnish

QUICK HOLLANDAISE

1tbsp lemon juice
1tbsp white wine vinegar
4 egg yolks, at room temperature
150g (5oz) unsalted butter, melted

1 Cut any woody ends off the asparagus and discard. Lay the spears flat in salted boiling water in a shallow pan (a sauté pan or frying pan is ideal), and simmer gently for 5–6 minutes until the asparagus is tender but still firm.

2 Meanwhile, make the quick hollandaise: three-quarters fill a food processor or blender with hot water from the kettle and pulse or process briefly, to warm the bowl. Pour the water away and dry the bowl.

3 Put the lemon juice and vinegar into the warm bowl of food processor or blender, add the egg yolks and pulse or process briefly.

4 With the machine running, gradually pour in the melted butter, and work until thick and creamy. Season to taste.

5 To serve, drain the asparagus. Ladle some of the hollandaise sauce on to warmed plates, arrange the asparagus on top, and garnish with lemon twists. Serve the remaining sauce separately.

DOUBLE SALMON TIAN

SERVES 6

650g (1lb 5oz) fresh salmon
 fillet, skinned
200g (7oz) low-fat soft cheese
4tbsp chopped fresh dill
salt and black pepper

TO SERVE

50–60g (1½–2oz) fresh mizuna
 leaves, or any other peppery
 leaves such as rocket
6 small slices of smoked salmon,
 total weight about 200g (7oz)
6 lemon wedges to serve
6 x 6.5cm (2¾in) metal rings or
 150ml (5fl oz) ramekin dishes

1 Wrap the fresh salmon tightly in foil and bake in a preheated oven at 190°C (375°F, Gas 5) for 15–20 minutes or until just cooked. Leave to cool in the foil.

2 Mix the cheese and dill in a large bowl until smooth. Flake the cooled salmon into the bowl, including any fish juices and jelly, but discarding any bones. Season well with salt and pepper, and fold gently together.

3 Put the metal rings on a flat plate or baking tray (if using ramekins, line them with cling film). Divide the salmon and cheese mixture between them, smoothing the surface with the back of a metal spoon. Cover and refrigerate for at least 2 hours, overnight if possible.

4 To serve, divide the salad leaves between 6 plates. Lift a ring filled with salmon on to the leaves using a fish slice, then carefully ease off the ring. (If using ramekins, invert the salmon on to the leaves and gently remove the cling film.) Top each tian with a loosely curled piece of smoked salmon and serve with wedges of lemon for squeezing.

MOULES MARINIERE

SERVES 6

90g (3oz) butter
1 small onion, finely chopped
1 garlic clove, crushed
3kg (6lb) mussels, cleaned
450ml (¾ pint) dry white wine
6 parsley sprigs
3 thyme sprigs
1 bay leaf
salt and black pepper
1tbsp plain flour
3tbsp chopped parsley to garnish

1 Melt two-thirds of the butter in a large saucepan, add the onion and garlic, and cook gently, stirring occasionally, for a few minutes until soft but not coloured.

2 Add the mussels, wine, parsley, thyme, and bay leaf, and season with salt and pepper. Cover the saucepan tightly and bring to a boil.

3 Cook, shaking the saucepan frequently, for 5–6 minutes or until the mussels open.

4 Throw away any mussels that are not open. Transfer the open mussels to a warmed tureen or large serving bowl.

5 Strain the cooking juices into a small pan and boil until reduced by one-third.

6 Mix the remaining butter and the flour on a plate to make a paste (beurre manié).

7 Whisk the beurre manié into the cooking liquid, and bring to a boil, stirring constantly. Taste for seasoning, and pour over the mussels. Garnish and serve at once.

Healthy option

This classic recipe is made with a butter-and-flour beurre manié, which thickens the sauce. For a healthier option, cook the onion and garlic in 2tbsp olive oil and omit the flour. To compensate for the lack of thickening, boil the cooking liquid in step 5 until reduced by about half.

Fish & Seafood

LOBSTER TAILS WITH MANGO & LIME

SERVES 4

4 cooked lobster tails
90ml (3fl oz) dry white wine
250ml (8fl oz) double cream
1 small mango, peeled, stoned,
  and cut into cubes
grated zest and juice of 1 lime
30g (1oz) Parmesan cheese, grated

1 Remove the flesh from the lobster tails (see box, below), then cut each piece of lobster flesh in half lengthwise. Arrange the pieces of lobster flesh, cut side-side up, in a large shallow ovenproof dish.

2 Pour the white wine into a small saucepan and boil rapidly until it has reduced to about 2tbsp.

3 Add the cream to the saucepan and boil until the mixture has reduced to a coating consistency. Stir in the mango cubes and grated lime zest and juice.

4 Spoon the mixture over the lobster in the dish. Sprinkle with the Parmesan cheese and bake in a preheated oven at 220°C (425°F, Gas 7) for about 20 minutes, until hot and bubbling. Serve hot.

REMOVING THE FLESH FROM A LOBSTER TAIL

Hold the tail in 1 hand. With a pair of scissors, cut along both sides of the underside of the shell, towards the end, without damaging the flesh.

Pull back the underside of the shell, and lift out the lobster flesh, making sure it is all in 1 piece.

GRILLED TROUT WITH CUCUMBER & DILL

SERVES 4

1 cucumber, peeled
30g (1oz) butter
small bunch of fresh dill, chopped
salt and black pepper
juice of 1 lemon
4 x 375–425g (12–14oz) trout,
   cleaned
dill sprigs and fresh chives to garnish
dill cream sauce (see below) to serve

1 Cut the cucumber in half lengthwise and scoop out the seeds, then cut the flesh across into 5mm (¼in) slices. Melt the butter in a saucepan, add the cucumber, and cook gently for 2 minutes.

2 In a bowl, combine two-thirds of the cooked cucumber with the chopped dill, season with salt and pepper, and sprinkle with the lemon juice. Stuff the trout with the mixture.

3 Line a grill pan with foil. Arrange the trout on the foil, and put the remaining cucumber around them.

4 Grill the trout under a hot grill, 10cm (4in) from the heat, for 4–7 minutes on each side until the flesh flakes easily.

5 Garnish the trout with dill sprigs and fresh chives, and serve at once, with dill cream sauce handed separately.

DILL CREAM SAUCE

Purée 300ml (½ pint) single cream, 90g (3oz) butter, 1 egg yolk, the juice of 1 lemon, and 1tsp plain flour in a food processor until smooth. Transfer the mixture to a small saucepan and heat very gently, stirring constantly, until the sauce has thickened and will coat the back of a spoon. Add salt and pepper to taste, then stir in 2tbsp chopped fresh dill and 1tbsp snipped fresh chives.

Trout with almonds

Dip the trout in seasoned flour. Melt 60g (2oz) butter in a large frying pan, and cook the trout, in batches if necessary, for 6–8 minutes on each side until the fish is opaque and the flesh flakes easily. Drain on paper towels, and keep warm. Wipe the pan, melt 15g (½oz) butter, and fry 60g (2oz) flaked almonds until lightly browned. Add a squeeze of lemon juice, then pour the lemon and almond mixture over the trout. Serve at once.

SIMPLE FISH SUSHI

Making your own sushi is easy as long as you keep it simple, as here. The three different types of sushi shown are made from one batch of rice and just a few ingredients in addition to the fish. Presented in a stylish way, the finished result is stunning.

MAKES 20

2 sheets of nori (dried Japanese
  seaweed)
a bowl of vinegar water
prepared Simple Sushi Rice (see recipe,
  page 42)
a little wasabi (Japanese horseradish
  paste)
175g (6oz) canned white crabmeat,
  drained and flaked
½ cucumber, halved lengthwise, seeded,
  and cut into long thin strips
bamboo rolling mat

HOSO MAKI

1 Lay the rolling mat on a flat surface with one of the longest edges facing towards you. Lay one sheet of nori shiny side down on the mat.

2 Dip your hand in vinegar water, take a handful of the sushi rice, and spread it over the nori, leaving a 2.5cm (1in) gap along the edge furthest away from you.

3 Spread a thin layer of wasabi – about 1cm (½in) wide – lengthwise along the middle of the rice (from left to right). Cover the wasabi with half the crab, then put a strip of cucumber on either side of the crab.

4 Moisten the uncovered edge of the nori with a little cold water. Using the mat and starting from the edge nearest to you, roll the rice in the nori, squeezing it to make a tight roll. Seal the moistened edge around the roll, then wrap in cling film. Now make a second roll in the same way.

5 To serve, unwrap the rolls and cut each one into 10 pieces with a very sharp knife that has been dipped in cold water (trim off the ends first so you get neat slices).

clockwise from top: *Nigiri Sushi, Hoso Maki,*
Sushi Squares with Smoked Salmon.

SUSHI SQUARES WITH SMOKED SALMON

MAKES 40

a bowl of vinegar water (see box, next column)
prepared Simple Sushi Rice (see recipe, below)
4 thin slices of smoked salmon
a few strips of sushi pickled ginger (gari), from a jar
32.5 x 23cm (13 x 9 in) Swiss roll tin

1 Line the swiss roll tin with cling film (if you don't have a tin, cover a chopping board with cling film). Dip your hand in vinegar water, take a handful of the sushi rice, and press it into the tin, patting it level with your hand. Repeat with more handfuls of rice until the tin is full. Refrigerate for about 15 minutes until firm.

2 Turn the tin upside down on to a board and remove the cling film. Cut into about 40 small squares with a sharp, wet knife. Cut the smoked salmon into little strips to fit on each square and top with a little pickled ginger.

SIMPLE SUSHI RICE

SERVES 6

500g (1lb) sushi rice
4tbsp rice wine vinegar
50ml (2fl oz) Japanese rice wine (mirin or sake)
¼tsp salt

1 Put the rice into a sieve and rinse under cold running water, then tip it into a saucepan and pour in 750ml (1¼ pints) cold water. Bring to a boil, lower the heat, and simmer, covered, for 15 minutes or until all the water has been absorbed.

2 Remove the pan from the heat and cover it immediately with a tea towel and lid (this is to make sure no steam can escape). Leave for 10 minutes.

3 Mix together the vinegar, rice wine, and salt in a bowl and fold gently into the rice. Continue to cut and fold through the rice while cooling with a fan (it is important to cool the rice down quickly so that it remains sticky).

NIGIRI SUSHI

MAKES 10

10 raw tiger prawns, shells and tails on
salt
a little wasabi
a bowl of vinegar water (see box, below)
prepared Simple Sushi Rice (see recipe,
  page 42)
10 small metal skewers

1 Push a skewer lengthwise through each prawn so the prawn becomes straight. Boil for 1–2 minutes in salted water until pink and cooked, drain, and cool. Remove the skewers and gently shell the prawns, leaving the tails intact.

2 Make a slit down the length of the belly of each prawn (without cutting right through), and gently open the prawn out. Remove the black vein from the back.

3 Using your finger, spread a little wasabi along the middle of the slit in the belly. Dip your hand in vinegar water and take a small amount of rice, about the size of a small walnut. Shape the rice with your hand (it will be very sticky) so that it fills the slit on top of the wasabi, then reshape the prawn around the rice by squeezing. Turn the right way up to serve.

Cook's know-how

The secret of good sushi is to make a good sticky rice, which is very simple. Instructions are usually on the packet, but the recipe here includes a little rice wine for sweetness, and a little salt. To stop the rice sticking to your hand you will need a bowl of vinegar water (water with a little vinegar added). Always use sushi rice on the day it is made. After you have made all the sushi, you can refrigerate them for up to 24 hours until ready to serve.

SERVES 4

12 uncooked tiger prawns in their shells
olive oil for brushing
300ml (½ pint) dry white wine
1 garlic clove, crushed
4tbsp chopped parsley
lemon and tarragon to garnish

TARRAGON SAUCE

150ml (¼ pint) soured cream
4tbsp chopped fresh tarragon
1tsp Dijon mustard
squeeze of lemon juice
salt and black pepper

TIGER PRAWNS WITH TARRAGON SAUCE

1 Make the tarragon sauce: combine the soured cream, tarragon, mustard, and lemon juice, and season with salt and pepper.

2 Heat a heavy frying pan. Brush the prawns with oil, add to the pan, and cook the prawns over a high heat for 2 minutes or until pink.

3 Keeping the heat high, add 150ml (¼ pint) of the wine and the garlic. Boil rapidly for 2–3 minutes, then stir in 2tbsp of the parsley.

4 When the wine has reduced slightly, lower the heat, and add the remaining wine, and season with salt and pepper. Simmer for 5 minutes or until the prawns have released their juices into the wine.

5 Spoon the cooking juices over the prawns, sprinkle with the remaining parsley, and garnish with lemon and sprigs of fresh tarragon. Serve hot, with the tarragon sauce.

SERVES 4

2 x 560g (1lb 2oz) black bream,
  filleted and skinned
grated zest and juice of ½ lemon
salt and black pepper
150ml (¼ pint) water
butter for greasing
30g (1oz) mature Cheddar cheese,
  grated
broccoli, to serve
lemon zest and parsley sprigs
  to garnish

WHITE SAUCE

30g (1oz) butter
1tbsp plain flour
150ml (¼ pint) milk

CHEESE-TOPPED BAKED BREAM

1 Cut the black bream fillets in half lengthwise, and arrange them in a single layer in a large ovenproof dish.

2 Sprinkle the fish evenly with the grated lemon zest and season with salt and pepper. Pour the lemon juice and measured water over the fish fillets. Cover the dish with buttered foil.

3 Bake in a preheated oven at 160°C (325°F, Gas 3) for about 20 minutes until the flesh flakes easily.

4 Transfer the bream to a warmed flameproof platter, cover, and keep hot. Strain the cooking liquid and reserve. Increase the oven temperature to 220°C (425°F, Gas 7).

5 Make the white sauce: melt the butter in a small saucepan, add the flour, and cook, stirring, for 1 minute. Remove from the heat, and gradually blend in the milk and the reserved cooking liquid. Bring to a boil, stirring constantly until the mixture thickens. Simmer for 2–3 minutes. Taste for seasoning.

6 Pour the white sauce over the fish, sprinkle with the cheese, and bake in the oven for 3–5 minutes until bubbling and golden. Serve hot with broccoli, garnished with lemon zest and parsley sprigs.

SEA BASS WITH LEMON BUTTER SAUCE

SERVES 6

sunflower oil for greasing
1.1kg (2¼lb) sea bass, cleaned
    and filleted
4 tarragon sprigs
1 lemon, sliced
salt and black pepper
2tbsp dry white wine

LEMON BUTTER SAUCE

150ml (¼ pint) single cream
juice of ½ lemon
45g (1½oz) butter, melted
1 egg yolk
1tsp plain flour
white pepper
1tsp chopped fresh tarragon

1 Put a large piece of foil on to a baking tray and brush lightly with oil. Put the sea bass on to the foil, tuck 3 of the tarragon sprigs and all but 1–2 of the lemon slices inside the cavity, and sprinkle with salt and black pepper.

2 Season the outside of the fish, and lift up the sides of the foil. Pour the wine over the fish, then seal the foil into a loose parcel. Bake in a preheated oven at 200°C (400°F, Gas 6) for 30 minutes or until the flesh is opaque, and flakes easily.

3 Meanwhile, make the sauce: whisk the cream in a pan with the lemon juice, butter, egg yolk, and flour until mixed. Heat very gently, stirring constantly, until the mixture is thick enough to coat the back of a spoon. Season with salt and white pepper, and stir in the tarragon. Keep warm.

4 Remove the sea bass from the foil and arrange on a warmed serving dish. Pour over the cooking juices. Garnish with the remaining lemon slices and tarragon sprig, and serve at once. Serve the warm lemon butter sauce separately.

LEMON SOLE FLORENTINE

SERVES 4

4 large lemon sole, each cut into 4 fillets
  and skinned
juice of ½ lemon
salt and black pepper
45g (1½oz) butter
45g (1½ oz) plain flour
450ml (¾ pint) milk
750g (1½lb) spinach
30g (1oz) Parmesan cheese, grated
hot lemon bread to serve
  (see box, below)

Fillets of lemon sole are topped with a cheese sauce and baked on a bed of spinach, so they stay moist while cooking. Slices of hot lemon bread – an interesting variation of garlic bread – make an unusual accompaniment.

1 Sprinkle the lemon sole fillets with the lemon juice and salt and pepper. Fold the fillets in half widthways, and set aside.

2 Melt the butter in a saucepan, add the flour, and cook, stirring, for 1 minute. Remove from the heat and gradually blend in the milk. Bring to a boil, stirring constantly until the white sauce mixture thickens. Simmer for 2–3 minutes, then add salt and pepper to taste.

3 Wash the spinach and put into a pan with only the water remaining on the leaves. Cook for 2 minutes or until wilted. Drain well.

4 Stir half of the sauce into the cooked spinach and spoon into a shallow ovenproof dish. Arrange the sole on top. Pour the remaining sauce over the top and sprinkle with the cheese. Bake in a preheated oven at 200°C (400°F, Gas 6) for 30 minutes. Serve hot, with hot lemon bread.

HOT LEMON BREAD

Beat the grated zest of ½ lemon into 125g (4oz) softened butter, using a fork. Work in the juice of ½ lemon, and salt and pepper to taste. Cut 1 baguette into 1cm (½in) slices, leaving the slices attached underneath.

Spread the butter in between the slices, and a little on top. Wrap in foil and bake in a preheated oven at 200°C (400°F, Gas 6) for 20 minutes, opening the foil for the last 5 minutes to crisp the top.

BEST-EVER FRIED FISH

SERVES 4

3tbsp plain flour
salt and black pepper
1 large egg, beaten
30g (1oz) fresh white breadcrumbs
4 large plaice fillets, skinned
sunflower oil
lemon wedges to garnish

These plaice fillets are shallow-fried in a crisp coating of fresh breadcrumbs. This is far superior to a batter coating in both flavour and texture, and it protects the fish from the heat of the fat and keeps it moist, in the same way as batter.

1 Sprinkle the flour into a shallow dish and season with salt and pepper. Pour the beaten egg into another dish, and sprinkle the breadcrumbs into a third.

2 Lightly coat the fish fillets with breadcrumbs (see box, below).

3 Heat a little oil in a large frying pan, add the coated fillets, in 2 batches if necessary, and fry over a high heat for 2–3 minutes on each side until they are crisp, golden, and juicy inside.

4 Lift the fillets out of the frying pan with a fish slice and then leave to drain briefly on paper towels. Serve the fish at once, garnished with the lemon wedges.

COATING A FISH FILLET

Dip the fillet into the seasoned flour, to coat. Shake off any excess.

Dip the floured fillet into the beaten egg, letting any excess drain off.

Dip the fillet into the breadcrumbs, making sure it is evenly coated.

GOLDEN FISH CAKES

SERVES 4

500g (1lb) potatoes, cut into chunks
salt and black pepper
500g (1lb) cod, haddock or salmon fillets
(or a mixture of white fish
and salmon)
300ml (½ pint) milk
1 bay leaf
9 black peppercorns
60g (2oz) butter
4tbsp chopped parsley
finely grated zest of 1 lemon
dash of Tabasco (optional)
1 egg, beaten
175g (6oz) fresh breadcrumbs
sunflower oil for frying
tartare sauce (see box, below) to serve

1 Cook the potatoes in boiling salted water for 15–20 minutes until tender.

2 Meanwhile, put the fish into a pan with the milk, bay leaf, and peppercorns. Bring slowly to a boil, and simmer for 10 minutes or until the fish is just opaque.

3 Drain the fish, reserving the liquid. Cool the fish, then flake the flesh, discarding the skin and bones.

4 Drain the potatoes, put them in a bowl, and mash with butter and 3tbsp of the fish cooking liquid. Add the fish, parsley, lemon zest, Tabasco if using, and salt and pepper to taste, and mix well.

5 Shape the mixture into 8 flat cakes, 7cm (3in) in diameter. Coat with beaten egg, then with breadcrumbs.

6 Heat a little oil in a frying pan and fry the fish cakes, a few at a time, for 5 minutes on each side or until golden. Serve hot, with the tartare sauce.

TARTARE SAUCE

Purée 1 egg, 1½tsp sugar, ½tsp mustard powder, and salt and pepper to taste in a food processor or blender until smooth. Add 300ml (½ pint) sunflower oil, pouring in a steady stream, and purée until the mixture is very thick and all of the oil has been incorporated. Add the juice of 1 lemon, and purée. Transfer to a bowl, and stir in 1tbsp each chopped gherkins, capers, and parsley, and 2tbsp chopped fresh tarragon. Cover and leave to stand for at least 1 hour to allow the flavours to blend.

FRESH WAYS WITH SALMON FILLETS

Fresh salmon is inexpensive and available all year round, either wild or farmed. Quick, easy and light, these four recipes using salmon fillets can all be prepared in advance, making them perfect stress-free main courses for dinner parties.

SERVES 4

a little olive oil
4 x 150–175g (5–6oz) middle-cut
   salmon fillets, skinned
salt and black pepper

SAUCE

200ml (7fl oz) low-fat crème fraîche
about 5cm (2in) cucumber, peeled,
   seeded, and finely diced
4tbsp chopped fresh dill
pinch of caster sugar
1tbsp capers
a good squeeze of lemon juice

GRIDDLED SALMON TRANCHES

1 Heat a griddle pan until piping hot, and lightly oil a sheet of foil on a baking sheet. Lightly oil and season the salmon.

2 Cook the salmon in the hot pan on one side only for 1½ minutes until golden underneath. Transfer, cooked side up, to the foil and finish cooking in a preheated oven at 190°C (375°F, Gas 5) for about 10 minutes or until the salmon is opaque and the flesh flakes easily. Leave to cool.

3 Mix the sauce ingredients in a bowl with salt and pepper to taste. Cover and refrigerate. When the salmon is cold, cover and refrigerate too – for up to 12 hours.

4 To serve, let the salmon come to room temperature and serve with the chilled sauce spooned alongside.

clockwise from top: Griddled Salmon Tranches, Warm Honeyed Salmon Salad, Herb Roasted Salmon, Thai Chilli Salmon.

HERB ROASTED SALMON

SERVES 4

4 x 150g (5oz) salmon tail fillets, skinned
salt and black pepper
a little vegetable oil
125g (4oz) low-fat garlic and herb
  soft cheese

TOPPING

30g (1oz) fresh white breadcrumbs
30g (1oz) mature Cheddar cheese,
  grated
2tbsp chopped fresh flat-leaf parsley
finely grated zest of 1 lime
lemon wedges to serve
flat-leaf parsley sprigs to serve

1 Season the salmon on both sides with salt and pepper. Place on lightly oiled foil on a baking sheet and spread with the soft cheese, not going quite to the edges.

2 Mix the topping ingredients together, adding seasoning to taste, then sprinkle over the salmon. (You can prepare ahead to this stage, cover the salmon, and keep it in the refrigerator for up to 12 hours.)

3 Cook in a preheated oven at 220°C (425°F, Gas 7) for 15 minutes or until the salmon is opaque and the flesh flakes easily. Garnish with lemon and parsley.

THAI CHILLI SALMON

SERVES 4

4 x 150–175g (5–6oz) middle-cut
  salmon fillets, skinned

MARINADE

2tbsp fish sauce (nam pla)
finely grated zest and juice of 1 lime
1 large fresh red chilli, halved, seeded,
  and finely chopped
2.5cm (1in) piece of fresh root ginger,
  peeled and finely grated
a few fresh coriander stems, finely chopped
fresh coriander leaves to serve
1 lime, cut into wedges

1 Put the salmon fillets in a single layer in a shallow non-metallic dish, add the marinade ingredients and turn to coat. Cover and marinate in the refrigerator for 2–3 hours, turning the salmon once.

2 Lift the salmon from the marinade and cook under a preheated hot grill, 7.5cm (3in) away from the heat, for 5–6 minutes on each side until the salmon is opaque and the flesh flakes easily. Serve hot, with coriander and lime.

WARM HONEYED SALMON SALAD

SERVES 4

4 x 150–175g (5–6oz) middle-cut
  salmon fillets, skinned
3tbsp clear honey
1tbsp olive oil
juice of 1 lemon
about 2tbsp chopped fresh thyme
new potatoes, to serve

FOR THE SALAD

1 fennel bulb, thinly sliced
6 spring onions, thinly sliced
3tbsp extra virgin olive oil
1tbsp lemon juice
1tbsp clear honey
4tbsp Greek yogurt
salt and black pepper
1 Romaine lettuce, shredded
2tbsp chopped parsley
2tbsp snipped fresh chives

1 Make the salad. Mix the fennel and spring onions in a bowl with the olive oil, lemon juice, honey, yogurt, and seasoning. Toss the lettuce in a separate large salad bowl with the chopped fresh herbs and seasoning. Cover both bowls and refrigerate for about 1 hour.

2 Cut each salmon fillet into four lengthways – they will look like flat sausages. Toss in the honey and season well. Heat the oil in a large non-stick frying pan and pan-fry the salmon over a high heat for 2–3 minutes on each side or until just opaque. Take care when turning the salmon as it breaks up quite easily. Add the lemon juice and thyme to the pan and heat until bubbling.

3 Toss the fennel salad through the lettuce, then spoon the honeyed salmon on top. Serve warm.

CRISPY-TOPPED SEAFOOD PIE

SERVES 4

500g (1lb) cod fillet
300ml (½ pint) milk
1 bay leaf
2 leeks, trimmed and sliced
175g (6oz) broccoli, cut into florets
175g (6oz) cooked peeled prawns
15g (½oz) butter
15g (½oz) plain flour
salt and black pepper
250g (8oz) packet ready-made
  shortcrust pastry, well chilled
30g (1oz) Gruyère cheese, grated

1 Put the cod into a saucepan with the milk and bay leaf, bring slowly to a boil, and poach gently for about 10 minutes until the fish flakes easily.

2 Meanwhile, blanch the leeks and broccoli for 3 minutes in a saucepan of boiling salted water. Drain.

3 Lift out the fish, remove and discard the skin and bones, and flake the fish. Strain and reserve the milk.

4 Put the leeks and broccoli into a pie dish, and add the cod and prawns.

5 Melt the butter in a small saucepan, add the flour, and cook, stirring, for 1 minute. Remove from the heat and gradually blend in the reserved milk. Bring to a boil, stirring constantly until thickened. Simmer for 2–3 minutes. Season to taste and pour over the pie filling.

6 Grate the pastry, and sprinkle over the sauce. Sprinkle with the grated cheese. Bake in a preheated oven at 200°C (400°F, Gas 6) for 25–30 minutes. Serve at once.

TUNA TERIYAKI

SERVES 4

4 x 175g (6oz) tuna steaks, about
  2.5cm (1in) thick
2 spring onions, thinly sliced,
  to garnish

MARINADE

3tbsp dark soy sauce
2tbsp sesame oil
1tbsp Japanese rice wine or sweet
  sherry
3 garlic cloves, chopped
1tbsp caster sugar
1cm (½in) piece of fresh root ginger,
  peeled and grated

1 Make the marinade: put the soy sauce, sesame oil, rice wine, garlic, sugar, and ginger into a non-metallic dish. Add the tuna steaks to the marinade and turn to coat. Cover dish and marinate in the refrigerator for up to 4 hours.

2 Reserve the marinade. Cook the steaks under a hot grill, 7cm (3in) from the heat, brushing with the marinade, for 3–4 minutes on each side. Serve at once, garnished with spring onions.

Healthy note

Fresh root ginger, a key ingredient in Asian cooking, is known to have healing properties. It helps stimulate the circulation, fights coughs and colds, and relieves indigestion. It may also relieve rheumatism.

Barbecued salmon teriyaki

Cut 4 salmon fillets into 2.5cm (1in) cubes and marinate in the refrigerator for up to 4 hours, as in step 1, then thread on to kebab skewers. Cook over a hot barbecue, turning and brushing frequently with the marinade, for 6–8 minutes.

SEVERN SALMON

SERVES 6

6 x 175g (6oz) salmon steaks
butter for greasing
salt and black pepper
watercress sprigs to garnish

WATERCRESS SAUCE

300ml (½ pint) single cream
60g (2oz) watercress, trimmed
90g (3oz) butter, melted
1tsp plain flour
juice of l lemon
1 egg yolk

1 Arrange the salmon steaks in a single layer in a buttered roasting tin, and sprinkle with black pepper.

2 Cover tightly with foil, and bake in a preheated oven at 180°C (350°F, Gas 4) for 15 minutes or until the fish is opaque and flakes easily.

3 Meanwhile, make the watercress sauce: put the cream, watercress, butter, flour, lemon juice, and egg yolk into a food processor, season with salt and pepper, and purée until smooth.

4 Transfer the cream and watercress mixture to a small saucepan, and cook over a gentle heat, stirring, until the sauce thickens. Taste for seasoning.

5 Serve the salmon hot on a pool of watercress sauce, garnished with fresh sprigs of watercress.

Cook's know-how

You can vary this recipe by using boneless salmon fillets instead of steaks. They usually weigh about 150g (5oz), and can be chargrilled or pan-fried with a little oil – they will take 10 minutes at the most. Instead of watercress, you can use a small bunch of fresh dill or tarragon.

KOULIBIAC

SERVES 8–10

75g (2½oz) long grain rice
salt and black pepper
60g (2oz) butter, plus extra for greasing
1 large onion, chopped
1 x 400g (13oz) can chopped tomatoes,
  drained
500g (1lb) fresh salmon fillets, cooked
  and flaked
2tbsp chopped parsley
grated zest and juice of 1 lemon
500g (1lb) puff pastry
1 egg, beaten
60g (2oz) butter, melted, and
  juice of ½ lemon to serve
lemon wedges and watercress sprigs
  to garnish

This is a type of salmon kedgeree enclosed in crisp puff pastry, which makes an impressive dish for a dinner party or other special occasion. In Russia, its country of origin, there is a saying, "Houses make a fine street, pies make a fine table".

1 Cook the rice in boiling salted water for 12 minutes or until just tender.

2 Meanwhile, melt the butter in a saucepan, add the onion, and cook very gently for about 10 minutes until soft but not coloured. Add the tomatoes and cook for 15 minutes. Leave to cool.

3 Drain the rice thoroughly, and combine with the onion and tomato mixture, the flaked salmon, parsley, and lemon zest and juice. Season with salt and pepper.

4 Roll out 425g (14oz) of the puff pastry into a 28 x 40cm (11 x 16in) rectangle. Arrange the salmon mixture down the middle of the rectangle, leaving a 7cm (3in) border on each side. Brush the border with a little of the beaten egg, and wrap and decorate the koulibiac using pastry trimmings and glaze again.

5 Bake the koulibiac in a preheated oven at 220°C (425°F, Gas 7) for 30–45 minutes until golden.

6 Transfer to a serving dish, and pour the melted butter and lemon juice into the cuts. Serve in thick slices, garnished with lemon wedges and watercress.

Poultry & Meat

FRENCH ROAST CHICKEN

SERVES 4

a small bunch of tarragon or rosemary
90g (3oz) butter, softened, plus
    extra for greasing
1.7–2kg (3½–4lb) chicken
salt and black pepper
300ml (½ pint) chicken stock or
    giblet stock
4 heads of roast garlic
    (see box, below) to serve
a good splash of red or white wine

1 Put the bunch of herbs and 30g (1oz) of the butter into the cavity of the chicken. Tie the legs together with string. Weigh the chicken and calculate the roasting time at 20 minutes per 500g (1lb), plus an extra 20 minutes.

2 Rub the remaining butter all over the chicken and sprinkle with salt and pepper.

3 Put the chicken, breast-side down, into a small roasting tin. Pour the stock into the bottom of the tin, and cover the chicken with buttered greaseproof paper or foil. Roast in a preheated oven at 190°C (375°F, Gas 5) for the calculated time. At regular intervals, baste the chicken and turn it first on to one side, then on to the other, and finally on to its back.

4 Lift the chicken on a long fork. If the juices run clear then it is cooked. Transfer to a warm serving platter, and cover with foil.

5 Leave the chicken to rest for about 15 minutes, then carve and serve with the cooking juices, boiled in the roasting tin with some red or white wine.

ROAST GARLIC

Cut the stalk ends off 4 heads of garlic, arrange in an oiled baking dish, and drizzle a little olive oil over the tops. Cook in a preheated oven at 190°C (375°F, Gas 5) for 45–60 minutes. To eat, squeeze the soft cloves of garlic from the papery skins.

Italian roast chicken

Roast the chicken in a large roasting tin. Forty minutes before the end of the roasting time, add 1 trimmed and thinly sliced fennel bulb and 2 red onions, peeled and quartered lengthwise, to the tin.

MOROCCAN POUSSINS

SERVES 2

2 x 375g (12oz) poussins,
  spatchcocked

MARINADE

3tbsp olive oil
grated zest of 1 lime and juice
  of 2 limes
1 small onion, finely chopped
2–3 garlic cloves, crushed
2tbsp chopped fresh coriander
1tbsp paprika
2tsp curry powder
pinch of cayenne pepper
salt

1 Mix all the marinade ingredients, except salt, in a non-metallic dish. Turn the poussins in the marinade, cover, and marinate in the refrigerator for at least 3 hours (or overnight), turning occasionally.

2 When ready to cook, preheat the grill to hot, and sprinkle the poussins with a little salt.

3 Put the poussins, skin-side down, on a rack under the grill, 15cm (6in) from the heat, and grill for 15–20 minutes on each side, turning once and brushing with the marinade. Check the poussins are done by pricking with a fork – the juices should run clear, not pink or red. Serve hot or cold.

Cook's know-how

It is quick and easy to spatchcock poussins, but you can buy them ready spatchcocked at most supermarkets, especially during the barbecue season.

CHICKEN CACCIATORE

SERVES 4

SERVES 4

8 small chicken portions (4 drumsticks
  and 4 small breasts or 8 thighs)
plain flour for dusting
salt and black pepper
3–4tbsp olive oil
90g (3oz) streaky bacon or pancetta,
  cut into strips
1 large onion, chopped
1 small green pepper, halved, seeded,
  and diced
2 garlic cloves, crushed
250g (8oz) mushrooms, quartered
125ml (4fl oz) red or white wine
1 x 400g (13oz) can chopped tomatoes
75ml (2½fl oz) tomato purée
2tsp chopped fresh sage
4tbsp chopped parsley
grated zest of 1 lemon
2tbsp capers, chopped
fresh sage sprigs to garnish

1 Lightly dust the chicken pieces with flour seasoned with salt and pepper, and shake off any excess.

2 Heat half of the oil in a large frying pan, add the bacon and chicken, and cook for 10–12 minutes until browned all over. Transfer to a casserole with a slotted spoon, then pour off the fat from the frying pan.

3 Heat the remaining oil in the frying pan, add the onion, green pepper, and half of the garlic, and cook gently, stirring, for 5 minutes until soft but not coloured. Transfer to the casserole with a slotted spoon. Add the mushrooms, and cook for 2 minutes. Add to the casserole.

4 Pour the wine into the frying pan, and boil until reduced to about 4tbsp. Add to the casserole with the tomatoes, tomato purée, and the sage. Cover and cook in a preheated oven at 180°C (350°F, Gas 4) for 45 minutes or until the chicken is tender when pierced with a fork.

5 Combine the remaining garlic with the chopped parsley, lemon zest, and capers. Stir into the casserole, and taste for seasoning. Serve hot, garnished with sage sprigs.

CHICKEN POT PIE

SERVES 6

1kg (2lb) chicken
1.25 litres (2 pints) chicken stock
1 onion, quartered
1 celery stalk, thickly sliced
pared zest and juice of 1 lemon
2 carrots
2 waxy potatoes
45g (1½oz) butter
45g (1½oz) plain flour, plus
  extra for dusting
salt and black pepper
125g (4oz) frozen peas
500g (1lb) ready-made shortcrust pastry
beaten egg yolk for glazing
2 litre (3½ pint) pie dish

Cook's know-how

The chicken, vegetables, and sauce
need to be cold before covering
with pastry or the pastry will
become soggy. This is a good dish
to make ahead up to the end of
step 5, then all you have to do is
assemble the pie and bake it for
half an hour. You can make the
filling up to 24 hours ahead and
keep it covered in the refrigerator.

1 Put the chicken, stock, onion, celery, and lemon zest into a large saucepan. Bring to a boil, cover, and simmer for 30 minutes.

2 Add the carrots and potatoes, cover, and simmer for about 20 minutes or until the vegetables are cooked and the chicken is just tender. Remove the vegetables from the liquid and set aside. Leave the chicken to cool in the liquid.

3 Remove the meat from the chicken, and cut into bite-sized pieces, discarding the skin and bones. Dice the vegetables.

4 Skim the fat from the cooking liquid, then bring 600ml (1 pint) to a boil. Melt the butter in another pan, add the flour, and cook, stirring occasionally, for 1 minute. Stir in the hot stock, whisking until it comes to a boil and thickens. Add the lemon juice and season with salt and pepper.

5 Stir the chicken, diced vegetables, and peas into the sauce, turn into the pie dish, then leave to cool.

6 On a lightly floured work surface, roll out the pastry, then cut out the lid, fill the pie, and cover.

7 Bake in a preheated oven at 190°C (375°F, Gas 5) for 30 minutes or until the top is crisp and golden brown. Serve hot.

COQ AU VIN

SERVES 4

30g (1oz) butter
1tbsp sunflower oil
1.5kg (3lb) chicken, cut into
  8 serving pieces
125g (4oz) streaky bacon rashers,
  cut into strips
8 small shallots or pickling onions
250g (8oz) button mushrooms
30g (1oz) plain flour
300ml (½ pint) chicken stock
300ml (½ pint) red wine
1 bouquet garni
1 large garlic clove, crushed
salt and black pepper
2tbsp chopped parsley to garnish

1 Melt the butter with the oil in a large flameproof casserole. Add the chicken, and cook for 10–12 minutes until browned all over. Lift out and leave to drain on paper towels.

2 Spoon off any excess fat, then add the bacon, shallots or onions, and mushrooms, and cook over a high heat, stirring, until golden brown.

3 Lift the mixture out of the pan with a slotted spoon and leave to drain thoroughly on paper towels.

4 Add the flour to the pan, and cook for 3–5 minutes, stirring constantly until lightly browned. Gradually pour in the stock, then the wine, stirring until smooth.

5 Return the chicken, bacon, shallots, and mushrooms to the casserole, and add the bouquet garni, and garlic. Season with salt and pepper. Bring to a boil, cover, and cook in a preheated oven at 180°C (350°F, Gas 4) for 45 minutes or until the chicken is tender when pierced with a fork.

6 Sprinkle the chicken with the chopped parsley, and serve hot.

Healthy option
To reduce the fat content of this classic dish, skin the chicken before cooking, use 2tbsp oil and no butter, and half the amount of bacon (or omit it altogether).

TARRAGON CHICKEN WITH LIME

SERVES 4

60g (2oz) butter, softened
grated zest of 1 lime and juice
   of 2 limes
4 skinless, boneless chicken breasts
1tbsp chopped fresh tarragon
salt and black pepper
150ml (¼ pint) full-fat crème fraîche
lime segments and fresh tarragon
   to garnish

1 Put the butter into a bowl, and beat in the lime zest. Prepare the chicken breasts (see box, below).

2 Put the chicken breasts into a roasting tin. Sprinkle with the lime juice, tarragon, and salt and pepper, and roast in a preheated oven at 200°C (400°F, Gas 6) for 20 minutes or until the chicken is cooked through.

3 Transfer the chicken breasts to warmed serving plates and keep warm.

4 Put the tin on the hob, add 1tbsp water to the cooking juices, stirring to dissolve the sediment, and bring to a boil, stirring. Cook, stirring, for 1–2 minutes. Stir in the crème fraîche and heat gently until warmed through.

5 Serve the chicken with the sauce, and garnish each serving with the lime segments and fresh tarragon.

PREPARING THE CHICKEN

Make 3–4 deep diagonal cuts in each chicken breast with a sharp knife. Spread the top of each breast with one-quarter of the lime butter.

HERB GRILLED CHICKEN

SERVES 8

8 chicken portions (legs or breasts)

HERB BUTTER

90g (3oz) butter, softened
3tbsp chopped parsley
3tbsp snipped fresh chives
2 garlic cloves, crushed (optional)
salt and black pepper

1 Mix the butter with the parsley, chives, and garlic, if using, and a good pinch each of salt and pepper.

2 Spread the chicken with the butter, and put, skin-side down over a hot barbecue, or skin-side up under a hot grill, 10cm (4in) from the heat. Cook for 10 minutes on each side or until the juices run clear when the chicken is pierced.

Healthy option

Butter makes the chicken luscious and golden brown, but it is high in saturated fat and calories. You can reduce this by using half the amount of butter or 2tbsp olive oil. Skinning the chicken before cooking is another option.

Jamaican chicken

Substitute ½tsp crushed peppercorns (red, green, and black), 1tsp chopped fresh thyme, and 3 chopped spring onions for the parsley and chives.

Thai coriander chicken

Substitute 1–2tbsp chopped fresh coriander and 2tbsp Thai green curry paste for the parsley and chives.

Hot paprika chicken

Substitute 2tsp paprika and 2tsp mustard powder for the parsley and chives.

CHICKEN TIKKA

SERVES 4–6

750g (1½lb) skinless, boneless chicken
   breasts, cut into 2.5cm (1in) cubes
cucumber raita (see box, below)
   to serve

MARINADE

2tbsp plain yogurt
2tbsp tomato purée
1 small onion, finely chopped
2.5cm (1in) piece of fresh root ginger,
   peeled and grated
3 garlic cloves, crushed
1tbsp tamarind paste (optional)
1tbsp paprika
1tsp ground cumin
large pinch of cayenne pepper
4–6 metal skewers

1 Make the marinade: in a large bowl, combine the yogurt, tomato purée, onion, ginger, garlic, tamarind paste (if using), paprika, cumin, and cayenne pepper.

2 Toss the chicken in the marinade. Cover and marinate in the refrigerator for at least 2 hours (or overnight), stirring occasionally.

3 Thread the chicken on to skewers, put under a hot grill, 10cm (4in) from the heat, and grill for 3–5 minutes on each side or until cooked through. Serve hot, with raita.

CUCUMBER RAITA

Cut half a cucumber in half lengthwise. Scoop out the seeds, then coarsely grate the flesh into a sieve set over a bowl. Sprinkle with salt, and leave to drain for 10 minutes. Press hard to extract the juices.

Tip the cucumber into a bowl and add 1 x 150g (5oz) carton plain yogurt, 3 thinly sliced spring onions, 3 heaped tbsp chopped fresh mint, and pepper to taste. Stir well to combine. Serve chilled.

CHICKEN AND TURKEY SALADS

Lean, low-fat chicken and turkey teamed with fresh seasonal salad ingredients and vegetables make healthy meals for every day and special occasions, and if you buy ready cooked meat they are very quick to put together. These salads are good for buffets too, as most of the preparation can be done well in advance.

SERVES 6

500g (1lb) skinless, boneless cooked
　chicken
3 spring onions, finely sliced

SAUCE

5tbsp sunflower oil
3tbsp white wine vinegar
2tsp Dijon mustard
2–3tsp caster sugar, to taste
2 canned anchovy fillets, finely chopped
200ml (7fl oz) half-fat crème fraîche
1tbsp chopped fresh tarragon
1tbsp chopped parsley
salt and black pepper

TO SERVE

2 perfectly ripe avocados
juice of ½ lemon
1 bunch of watercress
2 spring onions, trimmed and cut
　lengthwise into fine slices

TARRAGON CHICKEN WITH AVOCADO

1 Cut the chicken into bite-sized pieces and mix with the spring onions in a bowl. Whisk all the sauce ingredients together in another bowl, adding salt and pepper to taste. Mix the sauce with the chicken, cover, and marinate in the refrigerator for at least 2 hours, overnight if possible.

2 Just before serving, halve, stone, and peel the avocados, slice the flesh into 1cm (½in) strips, and toss in the lemon juice. Gently mix the avocado into the salad, and spoon into a serving dish. Garnish with watercress and spring onions, and serve.

Clockwise from top: Tarragon Chicken with Avocado, Red Pepper Herbed Chicken Salad, Vietnamese Turkey Salad

VIETNAMESE TURKEY SALAD

SERVES 4

4tbsp fish sauce
500g (1lb) turkey breast steaks
4tbsp lime juice
1tbsp sugar, or more to taste
¼tsp ground black pepper
1 small fresh red chilli, halved, seeded, and finely chopped
250g (8oz) hard white cabbage, finely shredded
2 medium carrots, finely shredded
1 small onion, finely sliced
1 large bunch of fresh mint

1 Half fill a medium wok or deep frying pan with water, sprinkle in half the fish sauce and bring to a boil. Turn the heat down to a simmer, lower in the turkey breast steaks, and cover the pan with a lid. Simmer for 10 minutes or until the turkey is cooked through. Lift the turkey out of the water, and leave until cool enough to handle.

2 Meanwhile, mix the remaining fish sauce in a large bowl with the lime juice, 1tbsp sugar, the black pepper and chilli. Add the cabbage, carrots, and onion, and mix well.

3 Cut the turkey into bite-sized strips and roughly chop 2tbsp mint. Toss the turkey and chopped mint into the salad, and mix again. Cover and marinate in the refrigerator for 2–4 hours.

4 To serve, toss the salad again, then taste for seasoning and add more sugar if you like. Serve on a bed of the remaining mint leaves.

Illustrated on page 75.

RED PEPPER HERBED CHICKEN SALAD

SERVES 6

500g (1lb) skinless, boneless
  cooked chicken

SAUCE

1 bunch of fresh parsley
1 bunch of fresh basil
60g (2oz) red pepper in oil or
  brine (from a jar), drained
juice of 1 small lemon
2tsp caster sugar
90g (3oz) low-fat Greek yogurt
4tbsp low-fat mayonnaise
90g (3oz) half-fat soft cheese
salt and black pepper

TO SERVE

fresh basil
strips of red pepper
tossed salad leaves

1 Make the sauce. Put the parsley, basil, red pepper, lemon juice, and 2tsp sugar in a food processor and pulse for about 30 seconds until quite coarsely chopped. Add the yogurt, mayonnaise, soft cheese, and seasonings and pulse again for about 30 seconds. The sauce should be mixed but not finely chopped – it should have texture and flecks of herbs. Taste and add more sugar and seasoning if you like. (If you haven't got a food processor, coarsely chop the parsley, basil, and red pepper. Mix the other ingredients together, then mix in the chopped herbs and red pepper.)

2 Cut the chicken into strips, mix into the sauce, and turn into a shallow serving dish. Cover and leave in the refrigerator for at least 4 hours, or overnight, for the flavours to infuse.

3 Before serving, check the seasoning, and garnish with basil and strips of red pepper. Serve on a bed of tossed salad.

Illustrated on page 75.

CHICKEN SATAY

SERVES 4

4 skinless, boneless chicken breasts, cut
   into 2cm (¾in) pieces
flat-leaf parsley sprigs and coarsely
   chopped peanuts to garnish

MARINADE

90ml (3fl oz) dark soy sauce
juice of 1 lemon
3tbsp sunflower oil
2tbsp dark brown sugar
3 garlic cloves, crushed
3 spring onions, thinly sliced

SATAY SAUCE

250g (8oz) peanut butter
2 garlic cloves, crushed
175ml (6fl oz) water
30g (1oz) creamed coconut,
   coarsely chopped
1tbsp dark soy sauce
1tbsp dark brown sugar
1cm (½in) piece of fresh root
   ginger, peeled and grated
1tbsp lemon juice
cayenne pepper
salt and black pepper
12 bamboo skewers

In this traditional Indonesian speciality, the rich satay sauce made from peanuts and coconut complements the pieces of chicken tenderized by a tangy marinade. Serve as a starter or a buffet party dish.

1 Make the marinade: in a bowl, combine the soy sauce, lemon juice, oil, sugar, garlic, and spring onions.

2 Toss the chicken in the marinade. Cover and leave to marinate in the refrigerator for 30 minutes.

3 Soak the skewers in warm water for 30 minutes.

4 Make the satay sauce: heat the peanut butter with half of the garlic for 2 minutes. Add the water, creamed coconut, soy sauce, sugar, and ginger, and cook, stirring, for about 2 minutes or until the sauce is smooth.

5 Add the lemon juice and remaining garlic, and season with cayenne pepper, salt, and black pepper. Keep warm.

6 Thread the chicken pieces on to the skewers. Place under a hot grill, 10cm (4in) from the heat, and grill for 2–3 minutes on each side until cooked through.

7 Serve the chicken satay at once, garnishing the sauce with parsley sprigs and peanuts.

CHICKEN WITH SAGE & ORANGE

SERVES 6

6 boneless chicken breasts, with
the skin on
1tbsp plain flour
orange segments and fresh sage
leaves to garnish

MARINADE

300ml (½ pint) orange juice
1tbsp dark soy sauce
2 garlic cloves, crushed
2tbsp chopped fresh sage
1cm (½in) piece of fresh root
ginger, peeled and grated
salt and black pepper

1 Make the marinade: combine the orange juice, soy sauce, garlic, sage, ginger, and salt and pepper. Toss the chicken in the marinade, cover, and leave to marinate in the refrigerator for 20–30 minutes.

2 Reserve the marinade, and arrange the chicken breasts, skin-side up, in a large roasting tin.

3 Roast the chicken in a preheated oven at 190°C (375°F, Gas 5) for 10 minutes. Pour the reserved marinade over the chicken, and continue roasting for 10 minutes or until the chicken is cooked through.

4 Remove the chicken with a slotted spoon, and arrange on a warmed platter. Cover and keep warm.

5 Pour all but 2tbsp of the marinade into a jug, and reserve. Add the flour to the marinade remaining in the roasting tin, and mix to a smooth paste.

6 Put the roasting tin on the hob, and cook, stirring, for 1 minute. Gradually stir in the reserved marinade. Bring to a boil, simmer for 2 minutes, and taste for seasoning. Strain, pour a little around the chicken breasts, and garnish with the orange segments and fresh sage. Serve the remaining sauce separately.

STIR-FRIED CHICKEN WITH CRISP VEGETABLES

SERVES 4

4 skinless, boneless chicken breasts, cut
   diagonally into 5mm (¼in) strips
2tbsp mild curry powder
black pepper
8 spring onions
250g (8oz) carrots
3tbsp sunflower oil
175g (6oz) baby sweetcorn
175g (6oz) sugar snap peas
2–3tbsp lemon juice
2tbsp clear honey
2.5cm (1in) piece of fresh root
   ginger, peeled and grated
salt
125g (4oz) bean sprouts
noodles to serve

1 Put the chicken strips in a bowl with the curry powder and season with black pepper. Toss until the chicken is coated, then set aside while you prepare the vegetables.

2 Finely slice the white parts of the spring onions, reserving the green tops to garnish the finished dish.

3 Peel the carrots and cut them into matchstick-thin strips.

4 Heat 2tbsp of the oil in a wok or large frying pan. Add the chicken strips and stir-fry over a high heat for 3–4 minutes until golden brown.

5 Add the sliced spring onions, the carrot matchsticks, the whole baby sweetcorn, and the sugar snap peas, then add the lemon juice, honey, ginger, and a pinch of salt. Stir-fry over a high heat for 4 minutes or until the vegetables are tender-crisp and the chicken is cooked through.

6 Toss in the bean sprouts, and stir-fry over a high heat for 1–2 minutes until heated through. Taste for seasoning. Serve on a bed of noodles, and garnish with the reserved green spring onions.

CHICKEN STIR-FRY

SERVES 4

3tbsp sunflower oil
4 spring onions, sliced
2.5cm (1in) piece of fresh root
 ginger, peeled and grated
1tsp Chinese five-spice powder
½tsp crushed dried red chillies
3 carrots, thinly sliced
2 peppers (red and yellow), halved,
 seeded, and cut into thin strips
4tbsp dark soy sauce
2tbsp dry sherry mixed with 2tsp
 cornflour
4 skinless, boneless chicken breasts,
 cut into 1cm (½in) strips

1 Heat 1tbsp of the oil in a wok or large frying pan, add the spring onions, ginger, five-spice powder, and chillies, and stir-fry for 1 minute.

2 Add the remaining oil, then add the carrots and peppers, and stir-fry over a high heat for 2–3 minutes. Add the soy sauce, sherry mixture, and chicken strips, and stir-fry for 3–4 minutes.

3 Add 125ml (4fl oz) water and stir-fry for 1–2 minutes until the liquid boils and thickens slightly. Serve at once.

SERVES 4

2 cloves
2tsp cumin seeds
seeds of 4 cardamom pods
1tsp garam masala
pinch of cayenne pepper
2tbsp sunflower oil
4 skinless, boneless chicken breasts
1 large onion, finely chopped
2 garlic cloves, crushed
2.5cm (1in) piece of fresh root
   ginger, peeled and grated
salt and black pepper
300ml (½ pint) chicken stock
150ml (¼ pint) single cream
1 x 150g (5oz) carton plain yogurt
sultanas and whole almonds, blanched,
   shredded, and toasted
   to garnish

Cook's know-how

Cardamom comes in 3 forms: as
pods, whole seeds, and ground
seeds. As the seeds lose their
flavour quickly, it is best to buy
whole cardamom pods and remove
the seeds when you need them.

If you like, use 1 x 400g (14oz)
can coconut milk (either full-fat or
reduced-fat) instead of the stock
in step 4, and omit the single
cream in step 5. You can then
finish the curry with just a swirl
of yogurt and a scattering
of chopped fresh coriander.

FRAGRANT CHICKEN CURRY WITH ALMONDS

The spices in this recipe are among those used
in ready-made curry powders, but using your own
individual blend of spices gives a truly authentic
flavour to a curry. This is a creamy, mild dish – not
too hot or spicy.

1 Crush the cloves in a mortar and pestle with
the cumin and cardamom seeds. Mix in the garam
masala and cayenne.

2 Heat the oil in a flameproof casserole. Add the
chicken breasts, and cook for 2–3 minutes on each
side until golden. Remove with a slotted spoon
and leave to drain on paper towels.

3 Add the onion, garlic, and ginger to the pan, and
cook gently, stirring occasionally, for a few minutes
until just beginning to soften. Add the spice mixture
and season with salt and pepper, then stir over a
high heat for 1 minute.

4 Return the chicken to the casserole. Pour in the
stock, and bring to a boil. Cover and simmer gently
for 15 minutes or until the chicken is tender.

5 Stir in the cream and yogurt, heat through very
gently, then taste for seasoning.

6 Spoon the curry into a serving dish, and sprinkle with
the sultanas and toasted shredded almonds. Serve hot.

SERVES 6

3 skinless, boneless chicken breasts (about 125g / 4oz each), cut into thin strips

about 2tbsp sunflower oil

1 large red pepper, halved, seeded, and cut into strips

250g (8oz) button chestnut mushrooms, halved

2tsp cornflour blended with 5tbsp cold chicken stock or water

salt and black pepper

250g (8oz) bean sprouts

about 200g (7oz) pak choi, coarsely sliced

60g (2oz) roasted cashew nuts, salted or unsalted

1 large ripe mango, peeled and sliced lengthwise

chopped fresh coriander to serve (optional)

MARINADE

1tbsp soy sauce

3tbsp rice wine vinegar or white wine vinegar

3tbsp clear honey

CHINESE CHICKEN WITH MANGO

1 Put the chicken in a bowl with the marinade ingredients and mix well. Cover and marinate in the refrigerator for about 2 hours, more if time allows.

2 Heat 1tbsp oil over a high heat in a wok or large frying pan. Lift half the chicken from the marinade (reserving it), and stir-fry for 1–2 minutes until golden all over and nearly cooked. Remove the chicken and set aside, then repeat with the remainder.

3 Heat the remaining oil in the pan, add the red pepper and mushrooms, and stir-fry for 1–2 minutes.

4 Return the chicken to the wok. Stir the cornflour mixture and pour it into the wok, then add the reserved marinade. Season with salt and pepper and bring to a boil. Add the bean sprouts and pak choi, and stir-fry until the pak choi has just wilted, about 2 minutes. Stir in the cashew nuts and mango slices, and serve at once, sprinkled with chopped coriander if you like.

MARINATED BARBECUE CHICKEN

Smoke-scented, crisp-skinned, and with tender flesh, marinated chicken is full of delicious flavour when cooked on the barbecue. These three recipes use different parts of the bird, all cooked with the skin on for the juiciest results.

ORANGE & ROSEMARY

SERVES 4

4 chicken breasts, with the skin left on
a few rosemary sprigs

MARINADE

75ml (2½fl oz) olive oil
75ml (2½fl oz) white wine vinegar
juice of 1 orange
2tbsp clear honey
4 garlic cloves, crushed
salt and black pepper

ORANGE SALSA

2 oranges, peeled, segmented, and diced
1 red pepper, halved, seeded, and diced
¼tsp crushed dried red chillies
   (chilli flakes)
1tbsp clear honey

1 Combine the marinade ingredients in a shallow non-metallic dish. Add the chicken and turn to coat, then cover and leave to marinate in the refrigerator for up to 24 hours.

2 Lay the rosemary sprigs on the barbecue rack, put the chicken on top, and barbecue for 15–20 minutes until the juices run clear. Turn the chicken over several times during cooking, and baste or brush with the marinade.

3 Mix together the ingredients for the salsa. Serve the chicken breasts sliced diagonally, with the salsa alongside.

clockwise from top: Orange & Rosemary, Fruity Coriander, Yogurt & Mint

SERVES 4

8 chicken drumsticks, with the
  skin left on

MARINADE

75ml (2½fl oz) olive oil
juice of 1 lime
2tbsp mango chutney
2.5cm (1in) piece of fresh root
  ginger, peeled and grated
30g (1oz) fresh coriander, chopped
salt and black pepper

MANGO SALSA

1 ripe large mango, diced
1cm (½in) piece of fresh root
  ginger, peeled and grated
3 spring onions, finely chopped
1tbsp mango chutney
1tbsp lime juice

FRUITY CORIANDER

1 Combine the marinade ingredients in a shallow non-metallic dish. Slash the drumsticks, add to the marinade, and turn to coat. Cover and leave to marinate in the refrigerator for up to 24 hours.

2 Barbecue the drumsticks, turning and basting or brushing with the marinade, for 15–20 minutes or until the juices run clear.

3 Mix together the ingredients for the salsa. Serve the drumsticks hot, with the mango salsa alongside.

Illustrated on page 89.

YOGURT & MINT

SERVES 4

8 chicken thighs on the bone, with the
  skin left on
couscous salad (made with 100g cooked
  couscous, fresh mint, spring onions, red
  pepper, cherry tomatoes, and pine nuts
  tossed in vinaigrette dressing) to serve

MARINADE

4tbsp olive oil
juice of ½ lemon
3 garlic cloves, crushed
30g (1oz) fresh mint, chopped
150g (5oz) plain yogurt
¼tsp each ground cumin and turmeric
salt and black pepper

1 Combine the marinade ingredients in a shallow non-metallic dish. Add the chicken and turn to coat, then cover and leave to marinate in the refrigerator for up to 24 hours.

2 Barbecue the chicken, turning and basting or brushing with the marinade, for 15–20 minutes or until the juices run clear.

3 Serve the chicken thighs hot or cold, on a bed of couscous salad, or with couscous salad served separately in a bowl.

Illustrated on page 89.

Successful marinating

A marinade will give poultry or meat extra flavour before it is cooked over a barbecue, and it may help tenderize it at the same time. A marinade is a mixture of liquids and seasonings. There is always an acid such as lemon juice, wine, or vinegar, which helps make poultry or meat more tender.

An oil, such as olive, sesame, or sunflower, keeps the meat or poultry moist and carries the flavours of the seasonings into the food. Seasonings usually include salt and pepper, but all kinds of spices and herbs can be used as well. Marinades often include garlic, onions, and fresh root ginger, which

also add flavour. Allow enough time for large pieces of poultry or meat to pick up the flavour of the marinade. Smaller pieces will pick up the flavour more quickly. Turn the food in the marinade occasionally to ensure an even coating, and baste or brush with the marinade when barbecuing.

BACON-WRAPPED CHICKEN BREASTS

SERVES 6

6 skinless, boneless chicken breasts
4tbsp coarse-grain mustard
black pepper
18 streaky bacon rashers, rinds
   removed
snipped fresh chives to garnish

1 Spread both sides of the chicken breasts with the mustard, and season with pepper.

2 Take 3 bacon rashers, stretch them with the back of a knife, and arrange them side by side and slightly overlapping. Wrap a chicken breast with the bacon (see box, below). Repeat with the remaining bacon and chicken.

3 Place the chicken breasts with the bacon seam-side down in a roasting tin, and roast in a preheated oven at 190°C (375°F, Gas 5) for 25–30 minutes until the bacon is crisp and brown and the chicken cooked through. Serve at once, garnished with snipped chives.

WRAPPING A CHICKEN BREAST IN BACON

Place a chicken breast at one end of the overlapped bacon rashers, and then wrap the rashers diagonally (working from side to side) around the chicken to make a neat parcel.

Healthy option

Use the leanest bacon you can and trim off all the fat along the top edge of each rasher. Allow 12 rashers rather than 18 – it does not matter if some of the chicken peeps through.

TURKEY & LEMON STIR-FRY

SERVES 4

600g (1¼lb) turkey breast fillets, cut
    diagonally into 2.5cm (1in) strips
375g (12oz) courgettes
1 large green pepper
1tbsp olive oil
250g (8oz) baby sweetcorn
salt
chopped parsley and lemon twists
    to garnish

MARINADE

125ml (4fl oz) dry white wine
grated zest and juice of 1 large
    lemon
2tbsp olive oil
black pepper

1 Make the marinade: combine the wine, lemon zest and juice, oil, and season with pepper. Toss the turkey strips in the marinade, cover, and marinate in the refrigerator for at least 30 minutes.

2 Slice the courgettes thickly on the diagonal. Halve the green pepper and remove the seeds, then cut the pepper halves into long thin strips.

3 Heat the oil in a wok, add the courgettes, sweetcorn, and green pepper, and stir-fry over a high heat for 2 minutes. Remove with a slotted spoon, and keep warm.

4 Remove the turkey strips from the marinade, reserving the marinade. Add the turkey to the wok, and stir-fry in two batches over a high heat each for 2–3 minutes or until golden brown.

5 Pour the reserved marinade over the turkey and cook for 3 minutes or until tender. Return the vegetables to the wok, and heat through. Taste for seasoning. Serve at once, garnished with parsley and lemon twists.

TURKEY SCHNITZEL

SERVES 4

3tbsp plain flour
salt and black pepper
1 large egg, beaten
60g (2oz) fresh breadcrumbs
4 x 175g (6oz) turkey breast escalopes
2tbsp sunflower oil
15g (½oz) butter
lemon slices and chopped parsley
   to garnish

1 Sprinkle the flour on to a plate, and season generously with salt and pepper. Pour the beaten egg on to another plate, and sprinkle the breadcrumbs on to a third plate.

2 Coat each escalope with the seasoned flour, shaking off any excess. Dip each floured escalope into the beaten egg, then dip into the breadcrumbs.

3 With a sharp knife, score the escalopes in a criss-cross pattern. Cover and chill in the refrigerator for 30 minutes.

4 Heat the oil with the butter in a large frying pan. When the butter is foaming, add the escalopes, and cook over a high heat until golden on both sides.

5 Lower the heat and cook for about 2 minutes or until the escalopes are tender. Test the escalopes by piercing with a fine skewer: the juices should run clear.

6 Lift the escalopes out of the pan, and drain on paper towels. Garnish with lemon slices and chopped parsley, and serve at once.

Cook's know-how

If you can't find turkey breast escalopes, buy breast fillets. Put them between 2 sheets of cling film, and pound with the bottom of a saucepan until they are about 5mm (¼in) thick.

GUINEA FOWL WITH MADEIRA SAUCE

SERVES 6

2tbsp sunflower oil
2 x 1.25kg (2½lb) guinea fowl, cut
  into serving pieces
4 shallots, halved
1tbsp plain flour
600ml (1 pint) chicken stock
150ml (¼ pint) dry white wine
4tbsp Madeira
salt and black pepper
375g (12oz) seedless green grapes
150ml (¼ pint) double cream
chopped parsley to garnish

1 Heat the oil in a flameproof casserole, and cook the guinea fowl pieces in batches for a few minutes until browned all over. Lift out and drain. Lower the heat, add the shallots, and cook, stirring, for 5 minutes or until softened. Lift out and drain.

2 Add the flour, and cook, stirring, for 1 minute. Pour in the stock, and bring to a boil, stirring. Add the wine and Madeira, and season with salt and pepper. Add the guinea fowl and shallots, and bring to a boil. Cook in a preheated oven at 160°C (325°F, Gas 3) for 1 hour or until just tender.

3 Transfer the casserole to the hob, add the grapes, and cook for 5 minutes. Add the cream, and heat gently. Garnish with parsley and serve hot.

SERVES 4

2.5kg (5lb) duck, with any giblets
  reserved for stock
cranberry sauce to serve (see right)
watercress sprigs to garnish

CRANBERRY STUFFING

30g (1oz) butter
1 small onion, finely chopped
175g (6oz) fresh brown breadcrumbs
125g (4oz) cranberries
1tbsp chopped parsley
¼tsp ground mixed spice
salt and black pepper
1 egg, beaten

GRAVY

1tsp plain flour
300ml (½ pint) duck giblet stock
  (see right)
black pepper

Cook's know-how

If there are no giblets in the duck,
use chicken stock and add a splash
of port or sherry and some grated
orange zest to the gravy.

ROAST DUCK WITH CRANBERRIES

Many people like the flesh of roast duck breast
a little pink, but the legs need to be well cooked, or
they may be tough. To accommodate the difference,
serve the breast meat first, and return the duck to the
oven for 15 minutes to finish cooking the legs.

1 Make the cranberry stuffing: melt the butter in a
pan, add the onion, and cook gently for 3–5 minutes
until softened.

2 Stir in the breadcrumbs, cranberries, parsley, and
mixed spice, and season with salt and pepper. Bind
with the egg, and leave to cool.

3 Remove any fat from the cavity of the duck. Spoon
the stuffing into the neck end of the duck, secure the
skin flap over the stuffing with a small skewer, and
pat into a rounded shape. Put any leftover stuffing
into an ovenproof dish and set aside.

4 Prick the skin of the duck all over with a fork, and
rub salt and pepper into the skin. Place the duck,
breast-side down, on a wire rack in a deep roasting
tin, and roast in a preheated oven at 200°C (400°F,
Gas 6) for 25 minutes or until golden brown.

5 Pour off some of the fat from the tin to reduce
splashing. Turn the duck breast-side up, and roast for
another 20 minutes or until brown.

GIBLET STOCK

Giblets are not often found in birds, but they make a really good stock.

1 Put the giblets (the neck, heart, and gizzard but not the liver) in a stockpot or large saucepan and cook until lightly browned. Stir in 1 litre (1¾ pints) water (or previously made stock). Bring to a boil, skimming off any scum that forms on the surface.

2 Add 1–2 quartered, unpeeled onions, 1 chopped celery stalk, 1 chopped carrot, 1 bouquet garni, and a few black peppercorns. Simmer for about 1 hour. Strain, then cool, cover, and keep in the refrigerator for up to 3 days, or freeze for 3 months.

6 Reduce the oven temperature to 180°C (350°F, Gas 4), and roast the duck, without basting, for 1–1¼ hours. Cook any leftover stuffing with the duck for the last 40 minutes.

7 Test the duck by inserting a fine skewer into the thickest part of a thigh: the juices will run clear when it is cooked. Keep warm, uncovered, while you make the gravy.

8 Pour off all but 1tbsp of the fat from the roasting tin. Set the tin on the hob, add the flour, and cook, stirring, for 2 minutes. Pour in the stock, and bring to a boil, stirring until lightly thickened. Taste for seasoning, and strain into a warmed gravy boat.

9 Put the stuffing into a serving dish, carve the duck, and garnish with watercress. Serve with the gravy and cranberry sauce.

CRANBERRY SAUCE

Put 500g (1lb) fresh cranberries into a saucepan with 125ml (4fl oz) water. Bring to a boil and simmer for about 5 minutes, until the cranberries have begun to break down. Stir in 125g (4oz) caster sugar and simmer until the sugar has dissolved. Stir in 2tbsp port before serving. Serve hot or cold.

SERVES 4

4tbsp Dijon mustard
1tsp chopped fresh marjoram
4 rabbit portions
30g (1oz) butter
2tbsp olive oil
1 large onion, chopped
2 garlic cloves, crushed
90g (3oz) piece of smoked streaky
  bacon, cut into pieces
1tbsp plain flour
450ml (¾ pint) chicken stock
salt and black pepper
150ml (¼ pint) single cream
2tbsp chopped parsley to garnish

Cook's know-how

If you are making your own stock
and you do not have a carcass
from a whole bird, chicken wings
make a good base. It is better to
use peppercorns than ground
black pepper because prolonged
cooking can turn ground black
pepper bitter. Skim off fat with a
large spoon, soak it up with paper
towels, or cool and lift it off.

RABBIT WITH MUSTARD & MARJORAM

1 Mix the mustard and marjoram and spread over
the rabbit pieces. Place in a shallow dish, cover, and
leave to marinate in the refrigerator for 8 hours.

2 Melt the butter with the oil in a large flameproof
casserole. When the butter is foaming, add the
rabbit, and cook for about 5 minutes until browned
all over. Lift out and drain on paper towels.

3 Add the onion, garlic, and bacon to the casserole
and cook for 3–5 minutes. Add the flour and cook,
stirring, for 1 minute. Gradually blend in the stock
and bring to a boil, stirring until thickened.

4 Return the rabbit to the casserole, season with
salt and pepper, and bring back to a boil. Cover and
cook in a preheated oven at 160°C (325°F, Gas 3)
for 1½ hours or until the rabbit is tender.

5 Transfer the rabbit to a warmed platter and keep
hot. Boil the sauce for 2 minutes until reduced. Stir
in the cream, taste for seasoning, and spoon over
the rabbit. Garnish with parsley.

GAME PIE WITH FENNEL & CARROTS

SERVES 6

2tbsp sunflower oil
750g (1½lb) boneless game meat, cut into strips or dice
2 large carrots, sliced
1 fennel bulb, sliced
1 large onion, chopped
2tbsp plain flour
300ml (½ pint) game stock or chicken stock
150ml (¼ pint) red wine
1tbsp redcurrant jelly
salt and black pepper
plain flour for dusting
250g (8oz) ready made puff pastry
beaten egg for glazing
chopped parsley to garnish
2 litre (3½ pint) pie dish

1 Heat the oil in a large flameproof casserole. Add the game in batches and cook over a high heat until browned all over. Lift out and drain on paper towels.

2 Lower the heat, add the carrots, fennel, and onion, and cook, stirring occasionally, for 5 minutes or until softened. Add the flour and cook, stirring, for about 1 minute. Gradually pour in the stock and bring to a boil, stirring until thickened slightly. Add the game, wine, and redcurrant jelly, and season with salt and pepper. Cover tightly and simmer very gently for 1 hour until tender. Leave to cool.

3 Lightly flour a work surface. Roll out the puff pastry until 2.5cm (1in) larger than the pie dish. Invert the dish on to the dough and cut around the edge. Cut a long strip of pastry from the trimmings and press on to the rim of the pie dish. Reserve the remaining trimmings. Spoon in the game and vegetable mixture. Brush the pastry strip with water, top with the pastry lid, and crimp the edge with a fork.

4 Make a hole in the top of the pie to let the steam escape. Roll out the reserved pastry and cut shapes with a pastry cutter. Brush the shapes with beaten egg, and arrange on the pie. Glaze with beaten egg.

5 Bake the pie in a preheated oven at 200°C (400°F, Gas 6) for 25–30 minutes until the pastry is well risen and golden. Garnish with parsley.

BEEF WELLINGTON

SERVES 8

1.5kg (3lb) centre cut beef fillet, trimmed
salt and black pepper
2tbsp sunflower oil
45g (1½oz) butter
1 small onion, finely chopped
250g (8oz) flat mushrooms, finely chopped
175g (6oz) smooth liver pâté
400g (13oz) ready made puff pastry
1 egg, beaten
thin mushroom gravy to serve

Inside a puff pastry case is a succulent piece of prime beef and a rich stuffing of liver pâté and mushrooms. The pastry locks in all the juices and ensures none of the wonderful flavours are lost. Serve with a mushroom and red wine gravy.

1 Season the beef with black pepper. Heat the oil in a large frying pan, add the beef, and fry over high heat to seal.

2 Put the beef fillet in a roasting tin and cook in a preheated oven at 220°C (425°F, Gas 7) for 20 minutes for rare beef, 25 minutes for medium, or 35–40 minutes for well-done. Leave to cool completely.

3 Meanwhile, melt the butter in the frying pan, add the onion and mushrooms, and cook, stirring, for 3 minutes or until softened. Increase the heat to high, and cook until the excess moisture has evaporated. Turn into a bowl and leave to cool completely.

4 Add the liver pâté to the mushroom and onion mixture, season with salt and pepper, and stir well to combine. Coat the mixture around the beef.

5 Wrap the beef in the pastry. Bake at 220°C (425°F, Gas 7) for 45 minutes or until the pastry is crisp and golden. Cover with foil after 30 minutes to prevent the pastry becoming too brown. Leave to stand for about 10 minutes, then slice and serve with the gravy.

Individual beef wellingtons

Cut the raw beef into 8 slices. Brown the slices in a frying pan, cool, then wrap each one in pastry with a little of the pâté mixture. Bake for 25–30 minutes.

BEEF STROGANOFF

SERVES 6

30g (1oz) butter
1tbsp sunflower oil
750g (1½lb) rump steak, trimmed and
    cut into strips (see box, below)
8 shallots, quartered
300g (10oz) button mushrooms, halved
salt and black pepper
300ml (½ pint) soured cream
chopped parsley to garnish

1 Melt the butter with the oil in a large frying pan. When the butter is foaming, add the steak strips, in batches if necessary, and cook over a high heat for 5 minutes or until browned all over. Remove from the pan with a slotted spoon.

2 Add the shallots and cook for about 10 minutes until soft and add mushrooms, and cook for a further 4 minutes.

3 Return the steak strips to the pan, and season with salt and pepper. Stir in the soured cream and heat gently. Garnish with parsley, and serve at once.

Healthy option

Stroganoff is a classic dish of steak pan-fried in butter and oil with mushrooms and soured cream, but there are ways of cutting down on the fat without compromising the flavours in the dish. Use a non-stick pan and omit the butter.

CUTTING THE BEEF

Slice the beef at an angle into thin strips, 5mm (¼in) wide and 5cm (2in) long, using a sharp chef's knife.

PEPPER STEAKS

SERVES 4

4 x 150–175g (5–6oz) fillet steaks,
    about 2.5cm (1in) thick, trimmed
salt and black pepper
2tbsp black peppercorns
30g (1oz) butter
1tbsp sunflower oil
2tbsp brandy
150ml (¼ pint) double cream
chopped parsley to garnish

1 Season the steaks on both sides with salt. Crush the peppercorns and spread them on a plate. Coat the steaks with the peppercorns (see box, below).

2 Melt the butter with the oil in a frying pan. When the butter is foaming, add the steaks, and cook over a high heat for 2 minutes on each side.

3 Lower the heat and continue cooking until the steaks are to your liking: rare steaks need 1 minute on each side, medium steaks 3 minutes on each side, and well-done steaks 4–5 minutes on each side. Lift out of the pan and keep warm.

4 Pour the brandy into the frying pan, and boil rapidly to drive off the alcohol. When the brandy has almost disappeared, stir in the cream, and add salt to taste. Gently reheat the sauce, pour it over the steaks, and garnish with parsley. Serve hot.

COATING STEAKS

Press each steak firmly on to the peppercorns, until both sides are well coated.

Healthy option

Instead of the classic brandy-creamy sauce, deglaze the pan with 2tbsp Madeira, port, or sherry, and make a gravy with 75ml (2½fl oz) each of red wine and stock. Season well.

MEXICAN BUFFET PARTY

Mexican food is ideal for an informal party where everyone helps themselves because it is the tradition in Mexico to put lots of different dishes on the table together rather than serving separate courses. Here there is something for meat eaters and vegetarians alike.

SERVES 4

6 x 150g (5oz) thick fillet steaks
2 roasted red peppers in olive oil (from a jar), cut into strips, with oil reserved
salt and black pepper
2 red onions, cut into chunky wedges
2 garlic cloves, coarsely chopped
2tbsp lime juice
fresh coriander to garnish

Guacamole

Roughly mash the flesh of 1 large ripe avocado in a bowl with a fork. Add ½ finely chopped onion, 1tbsp chopped fresh coriander, and the juice of 1 lime. Mix well, and season to taste. Chill for no more than 30 minutes before serving, or the avocado will discolour.

CHARGRILLED STEAKS WITH RED VEGETABLES

1 Heat a ridged cast iron chargrill pan over a medium heat until very hot. Brush the fillet steaks with a little of the reserved oil from the peppers, and season with salt and pepper. When the pan is hot, chargrill the steaks for about 3–4 minutes on each side for rare meat, 4–5 minutes on each side for medium, and 7–8 minutes on each side for well-done. Remove the steaks from the pan and leave to rest.

2 Turn down the heat under the pan to low, add the red onion wedges, and cook for about 5–8 minutes, turning them occasionally, until they are charred and softened. Add the red pepper strips, the garlic and lime juice, and stir-fry for 1–2 minutes until hot and sizzling. Season with salt and pepper.

3 Serve the steaks whole or sliced thickly on the diagonal, with a garnish of fresh coriander and the red peppers and onions spooned alongside.

clockwise from top: *Vegetarian Enchiladas with Guacamole, Refried Beans, Chargrilled Steaks with Red Vegetables, Mexican Bean Salad.*

VEGETARIAN ENCHILADAS

SERVES 6

4 large tortilla wraps, about 23cm
  (9ins) in diameter
1 x 175g (6oz) can red kidney
  beans, drained
60g (2oz) feta cheese, grated
60g (2oz) Cheddar cheese, grated
1tbsp olive oil

MEXICAN TOMATO SAUCE

1tbsp olive oil
½ small onion, finely chopped
1 green chilli, halved, seeded, and
  finely chopped
1 garlic clove, crushed
1 x 400g (14oz) can chopped
  tomatoes grated zest of ½ lime
2tbsp chopped fresh coriander
salt and black pepper

1 Make the tomato sauce. Heat the oil in a pan, add the onion, chilli and garlic, and fry over a high heat for a few minutes. Add the tomatoes and simmer without a lid over a low heat, stirring from time to time, for about 10 minutes until the mixture is fairly thick (the consistency of chutney). If it is still a little runny, reduce it by boiling over a high heat, stirring continuously. Add the lime zest and coriander, and season with salt and pepper.

2 Take one tortilla and spread half of the tomato sauce over it to within 2.5cm (1in) of the edge. Top with half of the red kidney beans, and sprinkle over half of both the cheeses. Put another tortilla on top and press down a little with your hand so the two tortillas are sandwiched together. Make a separate tortilla sandwich (enchilada) with the remaining ingredients.

3 Heat the oil in a frying pan with a wide base, so the tortillas can fit in flat. Fry each enchilada for 3–4 minutes on each side or until the tortillas are golden brown and crisp, the filling is hot, and the cheese melted. Slice each enchilada into 6 wedges to serve.

Illustrated on page 107.

MEXICAN BEAN SALAD

SERVES 6

350g (12oz) mixed dried beans, eg red
  kidney, haricot, black eye, and aduki,
  soaked in cold water overnight,
  or 2 x 400g (14oz) cans beans
3 celery stalks, finely chopped
1 red onion, finely chopped
2 garlic cloves, crushed

DRESSING

4tbsp olive oil
2tbsp lime juice
2tbsp chopped fresh coriander
1tsp Dijon mustard
1tsp clear honey
salt and black pepper

1 Heat the oil in a wok or large non-stick frying pan and stir-fry the chilli and ginger for 2 minutes. Add the curry paste and stir-fry for a further minute.

2 Add the cauliflower and beans and stir to evenly coat the vegetables in the spices. Pour in the coconut milk and stock, then add the lemon grass and seasoning. Bring to a boil and simmer gently for about 20–30 minutes until the beans and cauliflower are just cooked (take care not to overcook them). Add the water chestnuts for the last 5 minutes. Remove and discard the lemon grass, scatter over the coriander and serve with rice.

Illustrated on page 107.

Refried beans

Heat 1–2tbsp sunflower oil in a frying pan. Add ½ finely chopped onion, and cook for 8 minutes, until lightly browned. Add 1 crushed garlic clove, and cook for 2 minutes. Drain and rinse 1 x 400g (14oz) can red kidney beans, and add to the pan. Cook over a gentle heat until warmed through, mashing the beans with a potato masher or fork and adding 1–2tbsp water if necessary, to prevent sticking.

FAJITAS

This Mexican speciality features slices of steak marinated in spices and fruit juice. Serve with tortillas, avocado, soured cream, and pico de gallo relish.

SERVES 4

500g (1lb) piece of rump steak
8 tortilla wraps
chopped coriander to garnish
1 avocado, stoned, peeled, and diced
soured cream

MARINADE

juice of 1 orange and 1 lime
3 garlic cloves, crushed
2tbsp chopped fresh coriander
a few drops of Tabasco sauce
salt and black pepper

PICO DE GALLO RELISH

6 tomatoes, diced
10 radishes, coarsely chopped
5 spring onions, thinly sliced
1–2 green chillies, halved, seeded, and chopped
4tbsp chopped fresh coriander
juice of ½ lime

WARMING TORTILLAS

Sprinkle each tortilla with a little water, and stack the tortillas in a pile. Wrap the tortillas in foil and warm in a preheated oven at 140°C (275°F, Gas 1) for 10 minutes.

1 Make the marinade: in a large bowl, combine the orange and lime juice, garlic, coriander, and Tabasco, and season with salt and pepper. Turn the steak in the marinade, cover, and leave to marinate in the refrigerator overnight.

2 Make the pico de gallo relish: in a bowl, combine the tomatoes, radishes, spring onions, chillies, coriander, lime juice, and salt to taste. Cover and chill until ready to serve.

3 Remove the steak from the marinade and pat dry. Put the steak under a hot grill, 7–10cm (3–4in) from the heat, and grill for 3 minutes on each side for rare steak, 4 minutes for medium steak, or 5–6 minutes for well-done steak. Cover with foil and leave to stand for 5 minutes.

4 Meanwhile, warm the tortillas (see box, left).

5 Slice the steak, arrange on serving plates, and sprinkle with coriander. Serve with the tortillas, pico de gallo relish, diced avocado, and soured cream.

HUNGARIAN GOULASH

SERVES 6

2tbsp sunflower oil
1kg (2lb) braising steak, trimmed
  and cut into 5cm (2in) cubes
2 large onions, sliced
1 garlic clove, crushed
1tbsp plain flour
1tbsp paprika
600ml (1 pint) beef stock
1 x 400g (14oz) can tomatoes
2tbsp tomato purée
salt and black pepper
2 large red peppers, halved, seeded,
  and cut into 2.5cm (1in) pieces
4 potatoes, peeled and quartered
150ml (¼ pint) soured cream
paprika to garnish

1 Heat the sunflower oil in a large flameproof casserole, add the beef in batches, and cook over a high heat until browned.

2 Lift out the beef with a slotted spoon. Lower the heat slightly, add the onions and garlic, and cook gently, stirring occasionally, for a few minutes until soft but not coloured.

3 Add the flour and paprika and cook, stirring, for 1 minute. Pour in the stock and bring to a boil, stirring.

4 Return the meat to the casserole, add the tomatoes and tomato purée, and season with salt and pepper. Bring back to a boil, cover, and cook in a preheated oven at 160°C (325°F, Gas 3) for 1 hour.

5 Add the red peppers and potatoes and continue cooking for 1 hour or until the potatoes and meat are tender.

6 Taste for seasoning, and stir in the soured cream. Sprinkle with a little paprika before serving.

Healthy option

Soured cream is the classic finish for goulash, but to reduce the fat content of this dish you can omit it. To compensate for its richness, add 250g (8oz) chestnut mushrooms, sliced, in step 5, and stir in a good handful of chopped flat-leaf parsley with the soured cream in step 6.

BOEUF BOURGUIGNON

SERVES 6

2tbsp sunflower oil
1kg (2lb) braising steak, trimmed
  and cut into 5cm (2in) cubes
250g (8oz) thickly sliced smoked
  bacon,rinds removed, cut into strips
12 shallots
30g (1oz) plain flour
300ml (½ pint) red Burgundy
150ml (¼ pint) beef stock
1 bouquet garni
1 garlic clove, crushed
salt and black pepper
250g (8oz) button mushrooms

1 Heat the oil in a large flameproof casserole. Add the beef in batches, and cook over a high heat, turning occasionally, until browned on all sides. Remove with a slotted spoon and set aside to drain on paper towels.

2 Add the bacon and shallots and cook gently, stirring occasionally, for 3 minutes or until the bacon is crisp and the shallots are softened. Lift out and drain on paper towels.

3 Add the flour and cook, stirring, for 1 minute. Gradually blend in the wine and stock and bring to a boil, stirring until thickened.

4 Return the beef and bacon to the casserole, add the bouquet garni and garlic, and season with salt and pepper. Cover and cook in a preheated oven at 160°C (325°F, Gas 3) for1½ hours.

5 Return the shallots to the casserole, add the whole button mushrooms, and cook for 1 hour or until the beef is very tender.

6 Remove the bouquet garni and discard. Taste the sauce for seasoning before serving.

CHILLI CON CARNE

SERVES 6

250g (8oz) dried red kidney beans
2tbsp sunflower oil
750g (1½lb) braising steak,
    trimmed and cut into cubes
2 onions, chopped
2 fresh red chillies, halved, seeded,
    and finely chopped
1 garlic clove, crushed
1tbsp plain flour
900ml (1½ pints) beef stock
2tbsp tomato purée
4 squares of plain chocolate, grated
salt and black pepper
1 large red pepper, halved, seeded,
    and cut into chunks
chopped coriander to garnish

Quick chilli con carne

Substitute 1 x 400g (14oz) can red kidney beans for the dried beans, and minced beef for the braising steak. Simmer gently on the hob for 45 minutes.

1 Put red kidney beans in a large bowl, cover with cold water, and leave to soak overnight.

2 Drain the beans, rinse under cold running water, and drain again. Put the beans into a large saucepan. Cover with cold water, bring to a boil, and boil rapidly for 10 minutes. Lower the heat and simmer, partially covered, for 50 minutes or until the beans are just tender. Drain.

3 Heat the oil in a large flameproof casserole. Add the beef and cook in batches over a high heat for 5–7 minutes until browned. Lift out with a slotted spoon.

4 Lower the heat, add the onions, chillies, and garlic, and cook, stirring occasionally, for a few minutes until softened.

5 Add the flour and cook, stirring, for 1 minute. Add the stock, tomato purée, and chocolate, and season with salt and pepper. Return the beef to the casserole, add the beans, and bring to a boil. Cover and cook in a preheated oven at 150°C (300°F, Gas 2) for 1½ hours until almost tender.

6 Add red pepper and cook for a further 30 minutes. Taste for seasoning, and garnish with coriander.

BEEF FLORENTINE

SERVES 8

11 sheets of filo pastry
60g (2oz) butter, melted

BEEF LAYER

30g (1oz) butter
1kg (2lb) lean minced beef
1tbsp plain flour
1 x 400g (14oz) can chopped tomatoes
2tbsp tomato purée
2 garlic cloves, crushed
1tsp caster sugar
salt and black pepper

SPINACH & CHEESE LAYER

625g (1¼lb) spinach, tough stalks
   removed, roughly chopped
90g (3oz) mature Cheddar cheese, grated
90g (3oz) Gruyère or Emmental
   cheese, grated
125g (4oz) full-fat soft cheese
2 eggs, lightly beaten

PREPARING THE FILO TOPPING

Brush 3 of the filo pastry
sheets with melted butter and
layer them flat on top of the
spinach mixture. Arrange the
remaining 8 sheets over the
dish, brushing with butter
and scrunching each one up,
to completely cover the lower
layer of filo pastry.

Filo provides a quick and easy way to cover a pie, and it gives a lovely crisp topping. If you prefer not to use butter you can use olive oil instead and, to make a lighter dish, you can use reduced-fat Cheddar cheese and low-fat soft cheese, and omit the Gruyère or Emmental.

1 Prepare the beef layer: melt the butter in a large saucepan, add the minced beef, and cook, stirring, for 10–15 minutes or until the meat is browned all over.

2 Add the flour and cook, stirring, for 1 minute. Add the tomatoes, tomato purée, garlic, and sugar, season with salt and pepper, and bring to a boil. Cover and simmer, stirring occasionally, for 35 minutes. Taste for seasoning.

3 Meanwhile, prepare the spinach and cheese layer: wash the spinach and put it into a large saucepan. Cook over a gentle heat until the spinach wilts. Drain thoroughly, squeezing to remove excess water. Mix the spinach with the Cheddar, Gruyère, soft cheese, and eggs, and season with salt and pepper.

4 Spoon the beef mixture into a shallow ovenproof dish, then spoon the spinach mixture over the top.

5 Prepare the filo topping (see box, left).

6 Bake in a preheated oven at 200°C (400°F, Gas 6) for 20–25 minutes until the filo pastry is crisp and golden. Serve hot.

LATIMER BEEF WITH HORSERADISH

SERVES 6

2tbsp sunflower oil
1kg (2lb) braising steak, trimmed and
   cut into strips
12 shallots or button onions
30g (1oz) plain flour
2tsp mild curry powder
2tsp light muscovado sugar
1tsp ground ginger
600ml (1 pint) beef stock
2tbsp Worcestershire sauce
salt and black pepper
3tbsp chopped parsley
4tbsp creamed horseradish
extra chopped parsley to garnish

1 Heat the sunflower oil in a large flameproof casserole, and cook the beef strips over a high heat until browned all over. Lift out with a slotted spoon and drain on paper towels.

2 Lower the heat, add the shallots, and cook gently, stirring occasionally, for a few minutes until softened. Lift out with a slotted spoon and drain on paper towels.

3 Add the flour, curry powder, sugar, and ginger to the casserole and cook, stirring, for 1 minute. Pour in the stock and bring to a boil, stirring until smooth and thickened. Add the Worcestershire sauce, season with salt and pepper, and return to a boil.

4 Return the beef and shallots to the casserole and stir in the parsley. Bring back to a boil, cover, and cook in a preheated oven at 160°C (325°F, Gas 3) for 2–2½ hours until the meat is tender.

5 Stir in the horseradish cream, taste for seasoning, and garnish with parsley.

Healthy option

Creamed horseradish is a mixture of grated horseradish with vinegar, seasonings, and cream. For a less rich finish, use just 1tbsp bottled grated horseradish.

COTTAGE PIES WITH CHEESY POTATO TOPPING

SERVES 6

2 tbsp sunflower oil
1 large onion, finely chopped
1 celery stalk, finely chopped
1 large carrot, finely chopped
750g (1½lb) minced beef
2tsp plain flour
300ml (½ pint) beef stock
1 tbsp tomato purée
2 tbsp Worcestershire sauce
salt and black pepper
2 tbsp chopped fresh coriander

TOPPING

750g (1½lb) potatoes, cut into
  chunks
30g (1oz) butter
about 150ml (¼ pint) hot milk
125g (4oz) mature Cheddar
  cheese, grated

COVERING THE PIES

Spoon the mashed
potato on to the beef
mixture, and spread
over the top to cover
completely.

Score the surface of
the mashed potato,
using a fork, to make
a decorative topping.

The minced beef mixture can be made a day ahead of serving, and kept in the refrigerator overnight. If you prefer you can omit the cheese in the potato topping, and use olive oil instead of butter.

1 Heat the oil in a large saucepan, add the onion, celery, and carrot, and cook for 3 minutes. Add the minced beef, and cook for 5 minutes or until browned.

2 Add the flour and cook, stirring, for 1 minute. Add the stock, tomato purée, and Worcestershire sauce, season with salt and pepper, and bring to a boil. Cover and simmer, stirring occasionally, for 45 minutes. Remove from the heat and spoon into 6 individual ovenproof dishes, or 1 large dish. Leave to cool.

3 Prepare the potato topping: cook the potatoes in boiling salted water for 20 minutes or until tender. Drain. Add the butter and hot milk to the potatoes and mash until soft, then stir in the cheese and season with salt and pepper.

4 Cover the minced beef mixture with the mashed potato (see box, left). Cook in a preheated oven at 200°C (400°F, Gas 6), allowing 20–25 minutes for small pies, 35–40 minutes for a large one, until the potato topping is golden brown and the meat mixture is bubbling. Serve hot.

THE BEST BURGERS

**Burgers don't have to be made with plain minced beef, as these three recipes illustrate.
They are very quick and easy to make, and will keep in the freezer for up to three months.
If you want to be sure that the burgers are seasoned enough, take a teaspoonful of the raw
mixture and flatten it into a mini burger shape. Fry it for a minute, turning once, then taste
it to see if it needs more seasoning or flavourings. If it does, add more to the raw mixture.**

SERVES 6

500g (1lb) best-quality minced beef
1tbsp red Thai curry paste
2tbsp chopped fresh coriander
2.5cm (1in) piece of fresh root ginger,
   peeled and finely grated
salt and black pepper
1tbsp olive oil

BARBECUE SAUCE

Heat 1tbsp sunflower oil in a saucepan and
cook 1 finely chopped onion and 1 crushed
garlic clove until soft but not coloured. Add
1 x 400g (14oz) can chopped tomatoes, 2tbsp
water, 2tbsp lemon juice, 1tbsp brown sugar,
1tbsp Worcestershire sauce, 2tsp Dijon mustard,
½tsp each paprika and chilli powder, and salt
and pepper. Bring to a boil, and simmer for
20 minutes. Serve warm. or cold.

THAI BURGERS

1 Put the beef in a bowl with the curry paste, fresh
coriander, grated ginger and salt and pepper. Mix
together thoroughly.

2 Shape the mixture into six even-sized burgers. Put
on a large plate, cover and refrigerate for about 30
minutes (they will keep for up to 24 hours).

3 Heat the oil in a large non-stick frying pan or lightly
coat a preheated ridged griddle pan with a little oil.
Cook the burgers over a medium heat for about 3-4
minutes on each side until they are brown. They are
best served just pink in the middle, but they can be
cooked another minute or two on each side if you
prefer them more done than this.

4 Serve hot with barbecue sauce.

*clockwise from top: Lamb Burgers in pitta pockets
with tzatziki, Veggie Burgers with a fresh tomato
salsa, Thai Burgers with cucumber and carrot
sticks, and a coconut milk, coriander, and chilli dip.*

LAMB BURGERS

SERVES 4-8

1–2tbsp olive oil
1 small onion, finely chopped
1 garlic clove, crushed
500g (1lb) best-quality minced lamb
1tsp ground cumin
2tbsp chopped fresh mint
salt and black pepper

TO SERVE

4 warm pitta breads, halved
about 8tbsp tzatziki (ready made or
   see box, right)

1 Heat 1tbsp oil in a frying pan and cook the onion and garlic until completely softened – this can take up to 10 minutes. Allow to cool completely.

2 Mix the cooled onion and garlic with the remaining ingredients, then shape into 8 small burgers. Put on a large plate, cover and refrigerate for about 30 minutes.

3 Heat a non-stick frying pan or lightly coat a preheated ridged griddle pan with oil. Cook the burgers until browned and cooked through, about 3–4 minutes on each side. Serve in warm pitta pockets, with tzatziki.

Illustrated on page 121.

MAKING TZATZIKI

Put 150g (5oz) Greek yoghurt, the grated zest and juice of 1 lemon, I crushed garlic clove , 1tbsp chopped fresh mint, and salt and pepper into a small bowl. Mix well to combine, then taste for seasoning. Cover and chill until required.

VEGGIE BURGERS

SERVES 6

1 small red onion, finely chopped
3tbsp chopped parsley
1 x 400g (14oz) can cannellini beans, drained
1 x 300g (10oz) can red kidney beans, drained
60g (2oz) no-need-to-soak dried apricots, snipped into pieces
175g (6oz) carrots, grated
60g (2oz) Cheddar cheese, grated
salt and black pepper
30g (1oz) pine nuts, toasted
about 2–3tbsp olive oil

1 Purée the onion and parsley in a food processor until fairly smooth. Add the remaining ingredients, except the pine nuts and oil, and blitz until smooth. (If you haven't got a processor, mash the beans and mix with the other ingredients except the pine nuts and oil.) Season really well.

2 Add the toasted pine nuts and pulse the machine to mix them in. Shape the mixture into 12 small burgers. Put on a large plate, cover, and refrigerate for about 1 hour (they will keep for up to 24 hours).

3 Place the burgers on a grill tray lined with foil, under a hot grill 7cm (3in) from the heat. Brush the burgers frequently with oil, for 4 minutes each side until they are hot right through.

Illustrated on page 121.

LANCASHIRE HOT POT

SERVES 4

2tbsp sunflower oil
1kg (2lb) middle neck lamb chops, trimmed
3 lamb's kidneys, trimmed (see box, below), and halved
1kg (2lb) potatoes, cut into 5mm (¼in) slices
500g (1lb) carrots, sliced
2 large onions, chopped
1tsp caster sugar
salt and black pepper
1 bay leaf
1 rosemary sprig
a few parsley sprigs
600–750ml (1–1¼ pints) lamb or chicken stock, or water
chopped parsley to garnish

1 Heat the oil in a flameproof casserole, add the lamb in batches, and brown over a medium heat for 5 minutes. Remove and set aside. Add the kidneys and cook for 3–5 minutes. Remove and set aside.

2 Add the potatoes, carrots, and onions, and cook for 5 minutes. Remove from the casserole.

3 Make layers of lamb chops, kidneys, and vegetables in the casserole, sprinkling with the sugar and a little salt and pepper, and putting the herbs in the middle.

4 Top with a neat layer of potatoes. Pour in enough stock or water to come up to the potato layer. Cover tightly and cook in a preheated oven at 160°C (325°F, Gas 3) for 2 hours or until the meat and vegetables are tender.

5 Remove the casserole lid, increase the oven temperature to 220°C (425°F, Gas 7), and cook for 20–30 minutes to brown the potato topping. Sprinkle with parsley before serving.

LAMB'S KIDNEYS

1 (If using beef or veal kidneys, first separate them.) Carefully cut through any fine membrane around each kidney and use your fingers to peel it off.

2 Set each kidney round-side up and slice lengthwise in half (or leave attached at the base). With a pair of scissors, snip out the small fatty, white core and the tubes.

Country hot pot

Omit the kidneys, and substitute 250g (8oz) swede for half of the carrots. Layer the meat and vegetables with 60g (2oz) pearl barley.

ROAST LEG OF LAMB WITH RED WINE GRAVY

SERVES 4–6

2kg (4lb) leg of lamb
salt and black pepper
2tbsp chopped fresh rosemary
1tbsp plain flour
300ml (½ pint) lamb or chicken stock
90ml (3fl oz) red wine
2tbsp redcurrant jelly (optional)
dash of Worcestershire sauce (optional)
mint sauce (see box, below) to serve
rosemary and thyme to garnish

SCORING THE FAT

Score the fat in a criss-cross pattern using a small, sharp knife, making sure that only the fat is cut, and that the meat underneath remains completely untouched.

MINT SAUCE

In a small bowl, combine 3tbsp finely chopped fresh mint with 1–2tbsp caster sugar, to taste. Add 3tbsp white wine vinegar or cider vinegar and stir well to mix.

A rich gravy that incorporates all the flavoursome juices from the meat is traditional with roast lamb. Red wine boosts the gravy's flavour, and you can add a spoonful of redcurrant jelly too, plus a squeeze of lemon juice and a dash of Worcestershire sauce if you like.

1 Trim the skin and excess fat from the lamb. Score the fat (see box, left). Insert a meat thermometer, if using, into the middle of the meat. Put the lamb, fat-side up, on a rack in a roasting tin, and rub with salt and pepper and the rosemary.

2 Roast the lamb in a preheated oven at 200°C (400°F, Gas 6) for 20 minutes. Lower the oven temperature to 180°C (350°F, Gas 4) and roast for 20 minutes per 500g (1lb) for medium-done meat, 25 minutes per 500g (1lb) for well-done meat, until the meat thermometer registers 75–80°C (170–175°F), and the fat is crisp and golden. Remove the lamb, cover with foil, and leave to stand for 10 minutes.

3 Meanwhile, make the gravy: spoon all but 1tbsp fat from the tin. Put the tin on the hob, add the flour, and cook, stirring, for 1 minute. Pour in the stock and wine, and bring to a boil, stirring to dissolve any sediment. Add the redcurrant jelly and Worcestershire sauce, if you wish.

RACK OF LAMB WITH A WALNUT & HERB CRUST

SERVES 4–6

2 prepared racks of lamb
1 egg, beaten

WALNUT & HERB CRUST

30g (1oz) fresh wholemeal
  breadcrumbs
2tbsp parsley, chopped
2tbsp coarsely chopped walnut pieces
2 large garlic cloves, crushed
finely grated zest of 1 lemon
1tbsp walnut oil
salt and black pepper

WINE & GRAPE SAUCE

150ml (¼ pint) dry white wine
25g (1oz) flour
150ml (¼ pint) lamb or chicken stock
1tsp honey
125g (4oz) seedless green
  grapes, halved

COATING THE LAMB

Press half of the walnut and herb crust mixture on to the meaty side of each rack of lamb, using a palette knife.

Also called best end of neck, a rack of lamb usually has 6–8 bones, which are called cutlets. The bones should be scraped clean of all fat – this is called "French trimmed" by some butchers.

1 Brush the outsides of the racks of lamb with some of the beaten egg.

2 Prepare the walnut and herb crust: combine the breadcrumbs, parsley, walnuts, garlic, lemon zest, and oil, season with salt and pepper, and bind with the remaining egg. Chill for 30 minutes.

3 Coat the racks with the walnut and herb crust (see box, below), and put them crust-side up into a roasting tin. Cook in a preheated oven at 200°C (400°F, Gas 6) for 30 minutes.

4 Remove the lamb, cover with foil, and leave to stand in a warm place for 10 minutes. Meanwhile, make the sauce: spoon all but 3tbsp of the fat from the roasting tin, and whisk in the flour.

5 Set the tin on the hob, pour in the wine, and bring to a boil, stirring to dissolve any sediment from the bottom of the tin.

6 Add the stock and boil, stirring for 2–3 minutes, and add the honey. Taste for seasoning, strain into a sauce boat, and stir in the grapes. Serve with the lamb.

HERBED BUTTERFLY LAMB CHOPS

SERVES 4

4 butterfly lamb chops
1tbsp olive oil
black pepper
4 rosemary sprigs
4 mint sprigs
4 thyme sprigs

1 Place the lamb chops on a grill rack and brush each one with half of the oil. Sprinkle with black pepper and scatter with the herb sprigs.

2 Place the chops under a hot grill, 10cm (4in) from the heat, and cook for 4–6 minutes. Remove from the heat, lift off the herbs, and turn the chops over. Brush the chops with the remaining oil, replace the herbs, and grill for 4–6 minutes until done to your liking. Serve hot.

Cook's know-how

Butterfly chops are double-sided, cut from a saddle of lamb, or double loin. They are also known as Barnsley chops.

IRISH STEW

SERVES 4

1kg (2lb) main-crop potatoes, cut into 5mm (¼in) slices
2 large onions, sliced
1kg (2lb) middle neck lamb chops, trimmed
a few parsley stalks
1 thyme sprig
1 bay leaf
salt and black pepper
300–500ml (10–16fl oz) water
chopped parsley to garnish

1 Put half of the potatoes into a flameproof casserole, cover with half of the onions, then add the chops, parsley, thyme, and bay leaf, and season with salt and pepper. Add the remaining onions, then the remaining potatoes, seasoning each layer with salt and pepper.

2 Pour in enough water to half-fill the casserole, and then bring to a boil. Cover tightly and cook in a preheated oven at 160°C (325°F, Gas 3) for 2–2½ hours until the lamb and potatoes are just tender.

3 Remove the lid, increase the oven temperature to 220°C (425°F, Gas 7), and cook for 20–30 minutes to brown the topping. Sprinkle with parsley before serving.

LAMB TAGINE

SERVES 8

¼tsp saffron threads
150ml (¼ pint) hot water
3tbsp olive oil
1.5kg (3lb) boneless shoulder of lamb,
    well trimmed and cut into 2.5cm
    (1in) cubes
1 fennel bulb or 4 celery stalks, trimmed
    and sliced crosswise
2 green peppers, halved, seeded, and cut
    into strips
1 large onion, sliced
30g (1oz) plain flour
½tsp ground ginger
450ml (¾ pint) lamb or chicken stock
grated zest and juice of 1 orange
125g (4oz) ready-to-eat dried apricots
salt and black pepper
mint sprigs to garnish

1 Prepare the saffron (see box, below). Heat the oil in a flameproof casserole, add the lamb in batches, and cook over a high heat for 5 minutes or until browned. Lift out and drain on paper towels.

2 Lower the heat, add the fennel or celery, peppers, and onion, and cook gently, stirring, for 5 minutes.

3 Sprinkle the flour and ginger into the vegetables and cook, stirring occasionally, for 1 minute. Add the saffron liquid to the casserole, return the cubes of lamb, then add the stock and orange zest, and season with salt and pepper. Bring to a boil, cover, and cook in a preheated oven at 160°C (325°F, Gas 3) for 1 hour.

4 Add the orange juice and apricots and cook for about 30 minutes until the lamb is very tender. Taste for seasoning and garnish with mint sprigs before serving.

PREPARING SAFFRON

Put the saffron threads into a small bowl, add the measured hot water, and leave to soak for 10 minutes.

BACON-WRAPPED PORK IN VERMOUTH SAUCE

SERVES 6

2 pork fillets (tenderloins), about 375g (12oz) each, trimmed
2tbsp Dijon mustard
salt and black pepper
375g (12oz) streaky bacon rashers, rinds removed

VERMOUTH SAUCE

30g (1oz) butter
1tbsp olive oil
1 shallot, finely chopped
1tbsp plain flour
200ml (7fl oz) chicken stock
90ml (3fl oz) dry vermouth
125g (4oz) button or chestnut mushrooms, sliced

1 Spread the pork fillets with the mustard and season with salt and pepper. Stretch the bacon rashers with the back of a knife and wrap around the fillets (see box, below).

2 Place the fillets in a roasting tin and cook in a preheated oven at 220°C (425°F, Gas 7), turning the fillets halfway through cooking, for 30–35 minutes until the juices from the pork run clear and the bacon is crisp and golden.

3 Meanwhile, make the sauce: melt the butter with the oil in a small pan. When the butter is foaming, add the shallot, and cook gently until softened.

4 Add the flour and cook, stirring, for 1 minute. Gradually blend in the stock and vermouth. Bring to a boil, add the mushrooms, and simmer for 15 minutes.

5 Transfer the pork to a warmed platter. Spoon off the fat from the roasting tin and strain the juices into the sauce. Heat through and taste for seasoning. Serve with the pork.

WRAPPING PORK FILLETS

Overlap half of the bacon rashers on a work surface. Lay 1 pork fillet across the bacon and plait the rashers around the meat. Secure with a fine skewer. Repeat with the second pork fillet.

SERVES 4

1.25kg (2½lb) pork spare ribs
salt and black pepper
spring onions to garnish (optional)

SWEET & SOUR SAUCE

2.5cm (1in) piece of fresh root ginger,
  peeled and grated
2 garlic cloves, crushed
2tbsp soy sauce
2tbsp rice wine or dry sherry
2tbsp hoisin sauce
2tbsp tomato purée
1tbsp sesame oil (optional)
1tbsp caster sugar

SWEET & SOUR CHINESE SPARE RIBS

1 Lay the ribs in 1 layer in a roasting tin, season with salt and pepper, and cook in a preheated oven at 140°C (275°F, Gas 1) for 1½ hours.

2 Make the sauce: combine all the ingredients in a small pan and heat gently.

3 Spoon the sauce over the ribs, turning them to coat. Increase the oven temperature to 180°C (350°F, Gas 4), and cook for 25–30 minutes. Serve hot, garnished with spring onions if you like.

Cook's know-how

Spare ribs are excellent for a barbecue, but they are best partially cooked first or they will burn on the outside before the meat is properly cooked inside. Cook them in the oven as in step 1 and coat with the sweet and sour sauce, then cook over hot charcoal for 15 minutes on each side.

SERVES 6

6 boneless pork loin chops
3tbsp coarse-grain mustard
125g (4oz) demerara sugar
3 small oranges
90ml (3fl oz) orange juice
salt and black pepper

PORK CHOPS WITH ORANGES

1 Spread both sides of each pork chop with the mustard, and sprinkle one side with half of the demerara sugar. Arrange the chops, sugared-side down, in a single layer in a shallow ovenproof dish.

2 With a sharp knife, carefully peel the oranges, removing all the pith. Cut the oranges into thin slices.

3 Cover the chops with the orange slices. Pour the orange juice over the top, season with salt and pepper, and sprinkle with the remaining sugar.

4 Cook, uncovered, in a preheated oven at 200°C (400°F, Gas 6) for about 35 minutes, basting the chops occasionally, until cooked through. Serve hot.

CALF'S LIVER WITH SAGE

SERVES 4

2tbsp plain flour
salt and black pepper
500g (1lb) calf's liver, sliced
60g (2oz) butter
1tbsp sunflower oil
juice of 1 lemon
3tbsp roughly chopped fresh sage
sage leaves and lemon slices to garnish

1 Sprinkle the flour on to a plate and season with salt and pepper. Coat the liver slices in the seasoned flour, shaking off any excess.

2 Melt half of the butter with the oil in a large frying pan. When the butter is foaming, add half of the liver slices and cook over a high heat for about 1 minute on each side, depending on the thickness, until browned all over. Lift out with a slotted spoon and keep warm. Repeat with the remaining liver slices.

3 Melt the remaining butter in the pan, and add the lemon juice and sage, stirring to dissolve any sediment from the bottom of the pan. Pour the pan juices over the liver, garnish with sage leaves and lemon slices, and serve at once.

Cook's know-how

Overcooking liver will toughen it, so make sure that the butter and oil are really hot, then the liver will cook quickly.

Calf's liver with apple

Halve and slice 1 eating apple and add to the pan with the lemon juice and sage. Cook, stirring, for 3 minutes, and serve with the liver.

Vegetarian

SERVES 6

60g (2oz) butter, plus extra for greasing
1 onion, sliced
2 garlic cloves, crushed
1kg (2lb) floury potatoes, thinly sliced
375g (12oz) celeriac, peeled and thinly sliced
300ml (½ pint) single cream
150ml (¼ pint) milk
250g (8oz) ricotta cheese
3tbsp snipped fresh chives
salt and black pepper
2tbsp fresh breadcrumbs
3tbsp grated Parmesan cheese, plus extra for serving

POTATO, CELERIAC, & PARMESAN GRATIN

1 Melt the butter in a frying pan, add the sliced onion and crushed garlic, and cook gently, stirring occasionally, for 3–5 minutes until softened but not coloured. Lightly butter a large gratin dish.

2 Arrange the potatoes, celeriac, and the onion mixture in layers in the prepared gratin dish, finishing with a neat layer of potatoes.

3 In a large bowl, combine the cream, milk, ricotta cheese, and chives, and season with salt and pepper. Beat well together, then pour over the vegetables.

4 In a small bowl, combine the breadcrumbs and 3tbsp grated Parmesan cheese, and then sprinkle evenly over the potatoes.

5 Bake in a preheated oven at 180°C (350°F, Gas 4) for about 1 hour or until the potatoes and celeriac are tender and the top is golden brown.

6 Serve the gratin hot, sprinkled with extra grated Parmesan cheese.

ROAST VEGETABLES NICOISE

SERVES 4

750g (1½lb) courgettes, sliced
1 large red onion, thinly sliced
3 garlic cloves, crushed
4tbsp olive oil, more if needed
125g (4oz) black olives, pitted
2tsp dried mixed herbs
1tbsp capers
black pepper
250g (8oz) cherry tomatoes, halved
1tbsp shredded fresh basil

1 Put the courgettes, red onion, and garlic in an ovenproof dish, drizzle with 4tbsp oil, and toss to mix.

2 Arrange the black olives on top of the vegetables, then sprinkle with the herbs and capers, and plenty of pepper.

3 Roast in a preheated oven at 190°C (375°F, Gas 5) for 25 minutes, then add the tomatoes and roast for a further 20 minutes, checking occasionally to see if the surface is getting too dry. If it is, drizzle a little more olive oil over the vegetables.

4 Sprinkle the dish with the shredded fresh basil. Serve hot or cold.

AUBERGINE PARMIGIANA

SERVES 4–6

2 medium aubergines
2 eggs, lightly beaten
60g (2oz) plain flour
3tbsp olive oil, a little more
   if needed
1 large onion, chopped
2 garlic cloves, crushed
500g carton passata
2tbsp fresh basil
¼tsp caster sugar
salt and black pepper
250–300g (8–10oz) mozzarella
   cheese, sliced
50g (2oz) Parmesan cheese, grated

1 Cut the aubergines into 1cm (½in) slices. Dip into the beaten eggs, then into the flour, shaking off any excess.

2 Heat 1tbsp olive oil in a large frying pan, add the aubergine slices in batches, and cook for 3–4 minutes on each side until golden, adding more oil between batches if necessary. Lift out with a slotted spoon and drain on paper towels.

3 Heat another tablespoon of olive oil in a saucepan, add the onions, and cook gently until soft. Stir in the passata, garlic, and basil. Bring to a boil, then simmer for 10–15 minutes until thickened. Add the sugar and season with salt and pepper.

4 Spoon some of the tomato mixture into a shallow ovenproof dish and cover with a layer of aubergine slices, then with a layer each of mozzarella and Parmesan. Continue layering, finishing with tomato mixture, mozzarella, and Parmesan.

5 Bake in a preheated oven at 190°C (375°F, Gas 5) for 15–20 minutes until the cheese is lightly browned.

Healthy option

For a lighter version of this dish, omit the egg and flour coating for the aubergines in step 1. In step 2, lightly brush the slices with olive oil, and grill or chargrill them until golden brown on each side.

ITALIAN STUFFED COURGETTES

SERVES 4

4 large courgettes
30g (1oz) butter
2tbsp olive oil, plus extra for greasing
1 small onion, finely chopped
4 ripe tomatoes, finely chopped
4tbsp chopped fresh basil
salt and black pepper
2tbsp capers, drained and coarsely
   chopped
250g (8oz) Fontina cheese, grated

1 Cut the courgettes in half lengthwise. Scoop out the flesh and chop finely.

2 Melt the butter with 1tbsp of the olive oil in a saucepan.

3 When the butter is foaming, add the onion and cook gently, stirring occasionally, for 3–5 minutes until softened but not coloured.

4 Add the courgette flesh, tomatoes, and basil, and season with salt and pepper. Cook, stirring, for 5 minutes.

5 Brush the insides of the courgette shells with the remaining oil and arrange in a lightly oiled shallow ovenproof dish. Bake the shells in a preheated oven at 180°C (350°F, Gas 4) for 5–10 minutes.

6 Divide half of the tomato mixture among the courgette shells. Cover with the chopped capers and a thin layer of cheese. Spoon over the remaining tomato mixture and top with the remaining cheese. Return to the oven and bake for 10–15 minutes until the cheese topping is bubbling.

Cook's notes

Fontina cheese is an Italian firm-textured springy cheese made from unpasteurized cow's milk. It has a delicate flavour. Instead, you could use Jarlsberg cheese from Norway, if liked.

VEGETABLE CASSEROLES

Delicious, satisfying casseroles can be made from fresh vegetables whatever the season, particularly when herbs, spices, and flavourings are carefully chosen to complement their flavours. These recipes make hearty main courses, served with either hot crusty bread or boiled or steamed rice.

SERVES 4

175g (6oz) small new potatoes,
  scrubbed and halved
8 baby carrots, scrubbed and trimmed
2 red onions, cut into wedges
2 garlic cloves, sliced
salt and black pepper
about 2tbsp olive oil
a few rosemary sprigs
250g (8oz) cherry tomatoes
125g (4oz) French beans
1 small cauliflower, broken into florets
1 x 400g (14oz) can butter beans,
  drained
2tbsp balsamic vinegar
2tbsp coarse-grain mustard
a handful of chopped fresh herbs
  (eg parsley, chives, basil, chervil)

ROASTED VEGETABLE MEDLEY

1 Put the potatoes, carrots, onions and garlic in a roasting tin. Season and add the olive oil, then turn to coat. Tuck in the rosemary sprigs, and roast in a preheated oven at 190°C (375°F, Gas 5) for 40–45 minutes or until the vegetables are tender, stirring in the tomatoes about 15–20 minutes before the end.

2 Meanwhile, cook the French beans and cauliflower in boiling salted water for 4 minutes. Drain and set aside.

3 Mix the roasted vegetables with the French beans, cauliflower, and butter beans, then gently mix in the balsamic vinegar, mustard, and herbs. Serve hot.

Roasted vegetable gratin

Transfer the vegetables to an ovenproof dish. Sprinkle with 90g (3oz) grated Cheddar cheese mixed with 60g (2oz) fresh breadcrumbs. Return to the oven for about 10–15 minutes until golden.

clockwise from top: *Spicy Pumpkin Casserole, Mushroom Stroganoff, Roasted Vegetable Medley.*

MUSHROOM STROGANOFF

SERVES 4

20g (¾oz) dried mushrooms (porcini)
2tbsp olive oil
1 onion, chopped
1 garlic clove, crushed
500g (1lb) chestnut mushrooms
2 red peppers, halved, seeded,
    and sliced
2tsp paprika
salt and black pepper
30g (1oz) cornflour
300ml (½ pint) cold vegetable stock
1 x 400g (14oz) can artichoke
    hearts, drained
2tbsp dry white wine
1tbsp tomato purée
low-fat crème fraîche or plain yogurt
    to serve

1 Soak the dried mushrooms in 150ml (¼ pint) warm water for 20 minutes, then drain and reserve the soaking water.

2 Heat the oil in a flameproof casserole, add the onion and garlic, and cook for 3–5 minutes until softened.

3 Add the mushrooms, peppers, and paprika, and season with salt and pepper. Cook, stirring, for 5 minutes. Mix the cornflour and stock, add to the pan with the artichokes, wine, mushroom water, and tomato purée and bring to a boil. Simmer gently for 10–15 minutes. Taste for seasoning. Serve hot, with crème fraîche or yogurt.

Illustrated on page 149.

Mushroom vol-au-vent

When cooking the mushrooms, increase the heat to reduce and thicken the sauce. Warm through a ready made large vol-au-vent shell, and fill with the hot Mushroom Stroganoff.

SPICY PUMPKIN CASSEROLE

SERVES 4

2tbsp olive oil
2 onions, cut into wedges
2 potatoes, cut into 2.5cm (1in) cubes
2 parsnips, cut into 2.5cm (1in) cubes
500g (1lb) pumpkin, peeled and cut
   into 2.5cm (1in) cubes
1–2tbsp curry paste
375ml (13fl oz) vegetable stock
salt and black pepper
chopped fresh coriander to garnish

1 Heat the olive oil in a flameproof casserole. Add the onions and cook gently for 3–5 minutes or until softened.

2 Add the vegetable cubes, curry paste, and stock. Season and bring to a boil. Cover and simmer, stirring, for 20 minutes.

3 Remove the vegetables with a slotted spoon and transfer to a warmed serving dish. Boil the sauce until reduced and thickened. Spoon the sauce over the vegetables, garnish with coriander, and serve hot.

Illustrated on page 149.

Spicy pumpkin in a pie

Cool the vegetables and sauce, transfer to a pie dish, and top with ready rolled pastry. Bake at 190°C (375°F, Gas 5) for 15 minutes or until the pastry is cooked and the filling is hot.

VEGETABLE STIR-FRY WITH TOFU

SERVES 4

250g (8oz) firm tofu, cut into
  bite-sized pieces
2tbsp sesame oil
1tbsp sunflower oil
1 head of chicory, halved lengthwise
4 carrots, thinly sliced diagonally
5cm (2in) piece of fresh root ginger,
  peeled and grated
250g (8oz) shiitake mushrooms, sliced
8 spring onions, sliced into 2.5cm
  (1in) pieces
250g (8oz) bean sprouts
3tbsp toasted sesame seeds

MARINADE

3tbsp soy sauce
3tbsp dry sherry
1 garlic clove, crushed
salt and black pepper

1 Make the marinade: in a bowl, combine the soy sauce, sherry, and garlic, and season with salt and pepper. Turn the tofu in the marinade, cover, and leave to marinate at room temperature for at least 15 minutes.

2 Drain the tofu, reserving the marinade. Heat the sesame and sunflower oils in a wok or large frying pan, add the tofu, and carefully stir-fry over a high heat for 2–3 minutes, being careful not to break up the tofu. Remove from the wok with a slotted spoon and drain on paper towels.

3 Separate the chicory halves into leaves. Add the carrots and ginger to the wok and stir-fry for about 2 minutes. Add the mushrooms and spring onions and stir-fry for a further 2 minutes, then add the bean sprouts and chicory leaves and stir-fry for 1 minute.

4 Return the tofu to the wok, pour the reserved marinade over the top, and boil quickly until almost all of the marinade has evaporated and the tofu has warmed through. Generously sprinkle with the toasted sesame seeds, taste for seasoning, and serve at once.

MUSHROOM LASAGNE

SERVES 6

2tbsp olive oil
1 large onion, finely chopped
500g (1lb) mushrooms, sliced
2 large garlic cloves, crushed
30g (1oz) plain flour
2 x 400g (14oz) cans chopped
   tomatoes
1tbsp chopped fresh basil
1tsp caster sugar
salt and black pepper
500g (1lb) frozen whole leaf spinach,
   thawed and drained
White sauce, made with 90g (3oz) each
   butter and plain flour, 900ml (1½ pints)
   milk, and 1tsp Dijon mustard
300g (10oz) mature Cheddar cheese,
   grated
150g (5oz) no-precook lasagne
   sheets

1 Heat the oil in a saucepan, add the onion, mushrooms and garlic and cook for 10 minutes or until soft. Sprinkle in the flour and cook, stirring, for 1 minute.

2 Add the tomatoes, basil, and sugar, and season with salt and pepper. Cover and simmer for 20 minutes.

3 Make the white sauce: melt butter in a small saucean. Sprinkle in the flour, and cook, stirring, for 1 minute. Remove from the heat and gradually blend in the milk. Bring to a boil, stirring, until the mixture thickens. Simmer for 2–3 minutes. Add the Dijon mustard.

4 Season the spinach with salt and pepper. Taking 1 teaspoonful at a time, shape it loosely into 24 balls.

5 Spoon one-third of the mushroom mixture into a large ovenproof dish, and place 8 of the spinach balls on top. Cover with one-third of the white sauce and one-third of the cheese. Arrange half of the lasagne on top. Repeat the layers, finishing with cheese.

6 Bake in a preheated oven at 190°C (375°F, Gas 5) for 35 minutes or until the pasta is tender. Serve hot.

Healthy option

This is a luxury lasagne for a special occasion. For everyday, halve the amount of white sauce and cheese.

VEGETARIAN BAKES

It is often hard to find inspiration for vegetarian main meals, especially when you are entertaining meat eaters at the same time. These special "two-in-one" recipes are the perfect answer – the vegetarians in your party will love to have something cooked especially for them, while the meat eaters will enjoy a spoonful or two alongside their own main course.

MAJORCAN TUMBET CASSEROLE

SERVES 6

625g (1¼lb) baby new potatoes
500g (1lb) courgettes, thickly sliced
500g (1lb) Spanish onions, thickly sliced
500g (1lb) tomatoes, halved
3 fat garlic cloves, peeled and left whole
olive oil
salt and black pepper
3tsp chopped fresh rosemary
400ml (14fl oz) passata (sieved
   tomatoes)
Tabasco sauce
3 fresh thyme sprigs, plus extra to garnish
1.8 litre (3 pint) ovenproof dish, about
   20 x 28 x 5cm (8 x 11 x 2in)

1 Boil the potatoes in salted water for 15–20 minutes until not quite done. Drain and leave to cool enough to handle, then peel and cut in half. Toss the courgettes, onions, tomatoes, and garlic cloves in 2tbsp of olive oil and season well. Arrange cut-side down on a baking sheet or in a shallow roasting tin. Roast in a preheated oven at 220°C (425°F, Gas 7) for 30–40 minutes, turning once, until charred and soft.

2 Pick out the garlic, squash it with the back of a knife, and return it to the tin. Layer the vegetables in an ovenproof dish – first the potatoes with some seasoning and rosemary, 6tbsp passata, and a dash of Tabasco, then the onions, tomatoes, and courgettes with seasoning, rosemary, passata and Tabasco. Push 3 sprigs of thyme in near the top.

3 Bake in a preheated oven at 200°C (400°F, Gas 6) for 15–20 minutes, or at 170°C (325°F, Gas 3) for 30–40 minutes, until hot and bubbling. Before serving, replace the cooked thyme with fresh thyme.

clockwise from top: *Tuscan Cannelloni, Kilkerry Pie, Majorcan Tumbet Casserole.*

KILKERRY PIE

SERVES 6

90g (3oz) butter
500g (1lb) leeks, trimmed and
   thickly sliced
60g (2oz) plain flour
300ml (½ pint) apple juice
300ml (½ pint) milk
1tsp coarse-grain mustard
salt and black pepper
4 hard-boiled eggs, roughly chopped
150g (5oz) mature Cheddar
   cheese, grated
500g (1lb) potatoes, cut into 5mm
   (¼in) slices (not peeled)
5 sheets of filo pastry, each about
   25 x 38cm (10 x 15in)
shallow ovenproof dish, about 25cm
   (10in) square

1 Melt 60g (2oz) of the butter in a large frying pan, and cook the leeks for about 8–10 minutes until softened. Stir in the flour and cook for 1 minute, then gradually add the apple juice and milk, stirring constantly until boiling. It may look slightly curdled at this stage, but don't worry, it will come together. Reduce the heat, and simmer gently for 2–3 minutes. Add the mustard and season well.

2 Remove the sauce from the heat and stir in the roughly chopped eggs and the cheese. Now cook the potatoes in boiling salted water for 4–5 minutes until just tender. Drain, and mix into the sauce, then season, and pour into the dish.

3 Melt the remaining butter. Brush one of the filo sheets with butter and put it over the mixture in the dish, scrunching up the edges to fit. Repeat with the remaining filo sheets, scrunching up the last sheet before putting it on top of the pie. You can leave the pie for up to 6 hours at this stage, then bake it when you need it.

4 Bake in a preheated oven at 200°C (400°F, Gas 6) for 30–40 minutes until the filo is crisp and golden and the pie is hot right through.

Illustrated on page 157.

TUSCAN CANNELLONI

SERVES 4

8 sheets of fresh lasagne, or dried
  lasagne cooked according to packet
  instructions
500g (1lb) passata (sieved tomatoes) or
  ready made fresh tomato and basil
  pasta sauce
2–3tbsp grated fresh Parmesan cheese
a small handful of chopped fresh basil

FILLING

a little olive oil
2 shallots, finely chopped
1 garlic clove, crushed
2 x 300g (10oz) cans cannellini
  beans, drained
60g (2oz) sun-blushed or sun-dried
  tomatoes, snipped into pieces
150g (5oz) Dolcelatte cheese,
  roughly chopped
2 heaped tbsp chopped fresh basil
salt and black pepper
shallow ovenproof dish, about
  28 x 20cm (11 x 8in)

1 Make the filling: heat the oil in a small pan, and cook the shallots and garlic until soft. Allow to cool. Crush the beans with a fork so that most are mashed but a few still retain some shape, then mix them with the shallots and garlic, tomatoes, Dolcelatte, and basil. Season well, taste, and add more seasoning if necessary.

2 Lay the lasagne sheets flat, divide the filling between them, and roll up from the short ends to enclose the filling. Put the cannelloni seam-side down into an oiled or buttered ovenproof dish – they should fit snugly. Season, then pour over the passata or pasta sauce.

3 Cover and cook at 190°C (375°F, Gas 5) for 45–50 minutes until the pasta is cooked and the filling piping hot. (If pre-cooked pasta was used, bake for 25–30 minutes.) Scatter the Parmesan and basil over the top before serving.

Illustrated on page 157.

TOMATO & OLIVE TART

SERVES 8

3tbsp olive oil
2 large onions, coarsely chopped
3 garlic cloves, crushed
1 x 400g (13oz) can chopped tomatoes
1 x 140g (4¾oz) can tomato purée
2tsp chopped fresh basil
1tsp caster sugar
125g (4oz) vignotte or mozzarella
  cheese, grated
90g (3oz) pitted black olives
shredded fresh basil to garnish

POPPYSEED BASE

250g (8oz) plain flour
125g (4oz) butter
90g (3oz) poppyseeds
1tbsp light muscovado sugar
salt and black pepper
about 4tbsp cold water

1 Make the base: put the flour, butter, poppyseeds, and sugar in a food processor, season with salt and pepper, and pulse until the mixture resembles fine breadcrumbs.

2 Add the water and process until the mixture forms a ball. Turn out and knead lightly, then roll out to a 30cm (12in) round on a baking sheet and pinch the edge to form a rim. Prick the base all over with a fork and chill for 30 minutes.

3 Heat the oil in a pan, add the onions and garlic, and cook gently for 3–5 minutes until soft. Add the tomatoes, tomato purée, basil, and sugar. Season and bring to a boil. Boil for 5–7 minutes until thick. Leave to cool slightly.

4 Bake the poppyseed base in a preheated oven at 220°C (425°F, Gas 7) for 15 minutes. Spread the tomato mixture over the base, sprinkle with the cheese and olives, and bake for 15–20 minutes. Serve hot or cold, sprinkled with basil.

Cook's know-how

If you are short of time, use ready made shortcrust pastry instead of the poppyseed base. You will need a 500g (1lb) packet.

VEGETARIAN CURRIES

The cuisine of India, with its use of aromatic spices to enhance the flavour of vegetables and pulses, is one in which vegetarians can find a wide range of dishes to enjoy. The tradition of eating a selection of small dishes, accompanied by rice and breads, makes for well-balanced, nutritious meals.

SERVES 6

2tbsp sunflower oil
3tbsp curry paste
½tsp chilli powder
2.5cm (1in) piece of fresh root ginger, peeled and grated
1 large onion, chopped
2 garlic cloves, crushed
3tbsp mango chutney
1 small cauliflower, cut into florets
2 potatoes, cut into chunks
2 large carrots, sliced
2 red peppers, halved, seeded, and cut into chunks
1 x 400g (14oz) can chopped tomatoes
1 x 400g (14oz) can coconut milk
250g (8oz) green beans, chopped into short lengths
salt and black pepper
juice of 1 lime
fresh coriander leaves to garnish

NIRAMISH

1 Heat the oil in a large saucepan, add the curry paste and chilli powder, and cook, stirring constantly, for 1 minute. Add the ginger, onion, garlic, and mango chutney, and cook, stirring, for 3–5 minutes until the onion is softened but not coloured.

2 Add the cauliflower, potatoes, and carrots to the pan, and stir well to coat in the spices. Cook, stirring occasionally, for 5 minutes.

3 Add the red peppers, tomatoes, and coconut milk to the pan and bring to a boil, then add the beans and season with salt and pepper. Stir well.

4 Cover and simmer gently for 25–30 minutes or until all the vegetables are tender. Stir in the lime juice and taste for seasoning. Serve hot, garnished with coriander leaves.

clockwise from top:
Niramish, Sag Aloo, Dhal.

DHAL

SERVES 4–6

225g (8oz) green lentils
1 bay leaf
2tbsp vegetable oil
1 large carrot, chopped
1 large green pepper, halved, seeded,
    and chopped
1 large onion, chopped
1 garlic clove, crushed
1cm (½in) piece of fresh root ginger,
    peeled and finely grated
½tsp each ground cinnamon, cumin,
    and coriander
1 x 400g (14oz) can chopped tomatoes
salt and black pepper

1 Rinse and drain the lentils, put them into a large saucepan, and pour in enough cold water to cover. Bring to a boil and add the bay leaf, then cover and simmer for 30 minutes or until the lentils are tender. Drain and remove the bay leaf.

2 Heat the oil in the saucepan, add the vegetables, garlic, and ginger, and fry for 10 minutes, stirring occasionally. Add the lentils, ground spices, and tomatoes and cook gently for 10 minutes or until the carrot is soft.

3 Purée the mixture in 3 batches in a blender or food processor. Do not purée for longer than about 30 seconds for each batch because the dhal should not be too smooth – it should retain some of the texture of the lentils. Reheat in the rinsed-out pan, and add salt and pepper to taste.

Illustrated on page 163.

Accompaniments

- tomato and coriander relish
- yogurt and cucumber raita
- grated carrot salad
- mango chutney
- poppadoms
- basmati rice
- naan bread

SAG ALOO

SERVES 6

500g (1lb) new potatoes
salt
2tbsp sunflower oil
1tsp mustard seeds
1tsp cumin seeds
2 onions, sliced
3 garlic cloves, chopped
2.5cm (1in) piece of fresh root ginger,
  peeled and grated
1 small fresh green chilli, halved, seeded,
  and finely chopped
2tsp ground coriander
½tsp turmeric
250ml (8fl oz) water
500g (1lb) fresh baby leaf spinach
2tbsp lime or lemon juice
plain yogurt to serve

1 Cook the potatoes in a saucepan of boiling salted water for 10 minutes. Drain and leave to cool. Cut into bite-sized pieces and set aside.

2 Heat the oil in a large, heavy frying pan. Add the mustard and cumin seeds and cook, stirring, for a few seconds until they pop. Add the onions, garlic, ginger, and chilli and cook for about 5 minutes until soft.

3 Add 1tsp salt, the ground coriander, and the turmeric. Cook, stirring, for 1 minute. Add the potatoes and turn to coat in the spices, then pour in the water and bring to a boil. Cover and cook over a gentle heat for 15 minutes or until the potatoes are tender.

4 Remove the lid and stir in the spinach. Increase the heat and cook, stirring occasionally, for about 10 minutes or until the spinach wilts right down into the sauce. Stir in the lime or lemon juice and taste for seasoning. Serve hot, with yogurt.

Illustrated on page 163.

ORIENTAL VEGETARIAN DISHES

Vegetarians fare better in the East than they do in the West because vegetarianism has been popular there for so much longer than here, and there are so many more dishes to choose from. These recipes from Thailand, Japan, and China are just a small sample to inspire you.

JAPANESE NOODLE SOUP

SERVES 6

1.5 litres (2⅓ pints) miso soup (3 sachets)
1tsp five-spice paste or 1tsp five-spice
  powder mixed to a paste with
  a little water
300g (10oz) udon noodles (made from
  wheat flour)
250g (8oz) tofu, cut into
  1cm (½in) cubes
3 spring onions, trimmed and shredded

1 Make up the miso soup, bring to a boil and add the five-spice paste. Simmer for 5 minutes, then add the noodles and simmer for 2 minutes, gently separating them with chopsticks or a fork.

2 Add the tofu and heat through for 1 minute. Ladle into soup dishes and scatter over the shredded spring onions before serving.

clockwise from top: Firecracker Stir-fry with long-grain rice, Japanese Noodle Soup, Peking Tofu with Plum Sauce.

FIRECRACKER STIR-FRY

SERVES 4

250g (8oz) pak choi
2–3tbsp sunflower or sesame oil
250g (8oz) sugarsnap peas, trimmed
1 red pepper, halved, seeded, and cut
  into strips
1 yellow pepper, halved, seeded, and
  cut into strips
2–3 hot fresh red chillies, halved,
  seeded, and sliced
300g (10oz) shiitake mushrooms, sliced
2–3tbsp soy sauce
salt and black pepper
boiled or steamed long grain rice,
  to serve

1 Cut the leafy tops off the pak choi, shred the leaves coarsely, and reserve. Slice the stems in half, or into quarters if they are large.

2 Heat the oil in a wok or large frying pan. Add the peas, peppers and chilli and stir-fry over a high heat for about 3–4 minutes. Add the mushrooms and pak choi stems and continue to stir-fry for another 2–3 minutes.

3 When the vegetables are just about tender, add the shredded pak choi leaves with a dash of soy sauce. Taste and add salt and pepper if needed, plus more soy sauce if you like. Serve immediately, with rice.

Illustrated on page 167.

SERVES 6

sunflower oil, for frying
250g (8oz) tofu, cut into 1.5cm
  (just over ½in) cubes
18 Chinese pancakes
  (ready made)
6 spring onions, trimmed and cut
  into matchsticks
¼ cucumber, peeled, seeded,
  and cut into matchsticks

PLUM SAUCE

250g (8oz) dark red plums, halved
  and stoned
1 small cooking apple, peeled, cored,
  and sliced
1 fresh red chilli, halved, seeded,
  and finely chopped
90g (3oz) caster sugar
50ml (2fl oz) white wine vinegar

PEKING TOFU WITH PLUM SAUCE

1 Make the plum sauce. Put the plums, apple, chilli, sugar, vinegar, and 25ml (1fl oz) water into a pan. Heat gently to dissolve the sugar, then bring to a boil. Partially cover and simmer gently for about 30–40 minutes until the fruits have cooked down and only a little liquid remains. Remove from the heat and allow to cool.

2 Pour enough oil into a non-stick frying pan to cover the base. Heat until hot, then fry the tofu for 3–4 minutes until golden brown all over, turning carefully. Remove and drain on kitchen paper.

3 To serve, spread a pancake with a little plum sauce, top with a little crispy fried tofu, spring onions, and cucumber and roll up to eat.

Illustrated on page 167.

SPINACH & GRUYERE QUICHE

SERVES 4–6

30g (1oz) butter
1 onion, chopped
225g (8oz) fresh spinach leaves, shredded finely
125g (4oz) Gruyère cheese, grated
250ml (8fl oz) single cream or milk
2 eggs, beaten
salt and black pepper

SHORTCRUST PASTRY

125g (4oz) plain flour
60g (2oz) butter
about 1tbsp cold water
20cm (8in) flan dish or tin
baking beans

Making shortcrust pastry

Tip the flour into a bowl and rub in the butter lightly with your fingertips until the mixture looks like fine breadcrumbs. Add the water and mix with a round-bladed knife to form a soft but not sticky dough.

1 Make the pastry with the flour, butter, and water (see box, below). Wrap in cling film and chill for 30 minutes.

2 Roll out the pastry on a lightly floured work surface, and use to line the flan dish or tin. Prick the bottom of the pastry shell with a fork.

3 Line the pastry shell with a sheet of foil or greaseproof paper, and fill with baking beans (or rice or pasta if you have no beans). Place the flan dish on a heated baking tray and bake the shell in a preheated oven at 220°C (425°F, Gas 7) for 15–20 minutes, removing the foil and beans for the final 10 minutes to dry out the centre.

4 Meanwhile, make the filling: melt the butter in a frying pan, add the onion, and cook gently, stirring occasionally, until golden brown. Season with salt and pepper. Add the spinach and fry for a couple of minutes to wilt.

5 Spoon the onion and spinach into the pastry shell, and sprinkle the cheese on top. Mix the cream and eggs in a jug, season with salt and pepper, and pour into the pastry shell.

6 Reduce the oven temperature to 180°C (350°F, Gas 4), and bake the quiche for 25–30 minutes until the filling is golden and set. Serve warm or cold.

ROQUEFORT QUICHE

SERVES 4–6

90g (3oz) Roquefort or other
  blue cheese, crumbled
175g (6oz) low-fat soft cheese
2 eggs, beaten
150ml (¼ pint) crème fraîche
1tbsp snipped fresh chives
salt and black pepper

SHORTCRUST PASTRY

125g (4oz) plain flour
60g (2oz) butter
about 1tbsp cold water
20cm (8in) flan dish or tin
baking beans

Making shortcrust pastry

Tip the flour into a bowl and rub
in the butter lightly with your
fingertips until the mixture looks
like fine breadcrumbs. Add the
water and mix with a round-
bladed knife to form a soft but
not sticky dough.

1 Make the pastry with the flour, butter, and water
(see box, below). Wrap in cling film and chill for
30 minutes.

2 Roll out the shortcrust pastry, and use to line the
flan dish or tin. Prick the bottom of the pastry shell
with a fork.

3 Line the pastry shell with foil or greaseproof paper,
and fill with baking beans (or rice or pasta if you have
no beans). Place the dish or tin on a heated baking
tray, and bake in a preheated oven at 220°C (425°F,
Gas 7) for 15–20 minutes, removing the foil and
beans for the final 10 minutes.

4 Meanwhile, make the filling: mix the Roquefort
and low-fat cheese in a bowl, then beat in the eggs,
crème fraîche, and chives, and season with salt and
pepper. Take care not to add too much salt as blue
cheese is quite salty.

5 Pour the mixture into the pastry shell, reduce the
oven temperature to 180°C (350°F, Gas 4), and bake
the quiche for about 30 minutes until golden and set.
Serve warm or cold.

Pasta & Rice

PENNE WITH SPINACH & STILTON

SERVES 4

500g (1lb) penne
salt and black pepper
45g (1½oz) butter
2 large garlic cloves, crushed
250g (8oz) chestnut mushrooms, sliced
300ml (½ pint) double cream
90g (3oz) spinach, coarsely shredded
90g (3oz) blue Stilton cheese, crumbled
juice of ½ lemon
pinch of grated nutmeg

1 Cook the pasta quills in boiling salted water according to packet instructions.

2 Meanwhile, melt the butter in a large pan, add the garlic and mushrooms, and cook for 2 minutes, stirring occasionally. Stir in the cream and boil for 2–3 minutes until the mixture reaches a coating consistency.

3 Drain the pasta, add to the mushroom and cream mixture, stir well, and heat through. Add the spinach, Stilton cheese, lemon juice, nutmeg, and pepper to taste, and stir well to coat the pasta. Serve at once.

EASY PASTA SUPPER DISHES

Pasta is so popular with most people that you can never have enough recipes for tasty dishes to make with it. These three are delicious everyday meals and are also good for informal entertaining. Just accompany them with a green salad and some good bread.

SERVES 4

375g (12oz) fusilli tricolore
250g (8oz) asparagus tips, cut into
   5cm (2in) lengths
3tbsp olive oil
2 garlic cloves, crushed
90g (3oz) chestnut mushrooms, sliced
500g (1lb) ripe cherry tomatoes, halved
60g (2oz) sun-blushed or sun-dried
   tomatoes, each piece snipped
   into three
salt and black pepper

TO SERVE

30g (1oz) pine nuts, toasted
a small handful of fresh basil
   leaves, shredded

FUSILLI WITH DOUBLE TOMATOES

1 Cook the pasta in boiling salted water according to packet instructions until just tender, adding the asparagus 2 minutes before the end of cooking. Drain the pasta and asparagus together and refresh under cold running water. Drain well.

2 Heat the oil in a large frying pan, add the garlic and mushrooms, and fry over a high heat for a couple of minutes. Add both kinds of tomatoes and continue to stir-fry over a high heat until they are just heated through. Season well.

3 Quickly toss the pasta and asparagus through the tomato mixture in the pan until everything is hot, then scatter over the pine nuts and basil. Serve at once.

Healthy Note
Tomatoes contain vitamins C and E. More importantly, they are also a rich source of lycopene, a powerful antioxidant that can help protect the body from harmful free radical damage. Cherry tomatoes are also rich in antioxidants. All these ingredients make this recipe a perfect addition to a healthy diet.

clockwise from top: Red Hot Ragù, Rigatoni with Mushrooms & Rocket, Fusilli with Double Tomatoes.

RED HOT RAGU

SERVES 6

375g (12 oz) rigatoni or other
   tubular pasta
60g (2oz) Parmesan cheese,
   coarsely grated
3tbsp chopped parsley, or 175g (6oz)
   young spinach leaves, shredded

SAUCE

500g (1lb) good-quality pork sausages
   with herbs
a little olive oil
3 garlic cloves, crushed
2 small red chillies, halved, cored, and
   finely chopped
2 x 400g (14oz) cans chopped
   tomatoes
1 large onion, finely chopped
1 good tbsp sun-dried tomato purée
1tbsp chopped fresh basil
½–1tsp caster sugar,
   to taste
salt and black pepper

1 Make the sauce. Cut long slits in each sausage, remove the skins, and discard. Heat a little oil in a non-stick frying pan and add the garlic and sausagemeat. Fry over a medium heat for about 4–5 minutes, breaking the meat up with a wooden spatula until it is brown, with a minced pork consistency. Stir in the remaining sauce ingredients. Bring to a boil, cover, and simmer gently for 40–50 minutes or until the sausagemeat is cooked. Check the seasoning.

2 Meanwhile, cook the pasta in boiling salted water according to packet instructions until just tender.

3 Drain the pasta and mix it into the sauce in the pan with half the Parmesan, then check the seasoning again. Scatter the parsley and remaining Parmesan over individual servings.

NOTE: If using spinach, stir it into the bubbling sauce and cook for a couple of minutes until it wilts before adding the pasta and half the Parmesan.

Illustrated on page 177.

SERVES 6

375g (12oz) rigatoni or other
   tubular pasta
150ml (5fl oz) dry white wine
1 small onion, finely chopped
500g (1lb) mixed wild or cultivated
   mushrooms, such as shiitake, oyster,
   ceps, coarsely sliced
salt and black pepper
6tbsp double cream
4tbsp good-quality pesto (ready made
   or see box, below)
60g (2oz) rocket leaves, roughly chopped
coarsely grated Parmesan cheese,
   to serve

FRESH PESTO

Purée 60g (2oz) grated
Parmesan cheese, 1 garlic
clove, 60g (2oz) pine
nuts, 60g (2oz) fresh basil
leaves, and salt and
pepper to taste in a
food processor until
almost smooth.

Add 4tbsp olive oil
gradually, with the
blades turning, scraping
the side of the bowl
occasionally with a
rubber spatula to ensure
that all of the mixture
is incorporated.

RIGATONI WITH MUSHROOMS AND ROCKET

1 Cook the pasta in boiling salted water according to packet instructions until just tender.

2 Meanwhile, pour the wine into a large frying pan, add the onion and cook over a low heat until the onion has softened, about 10–15 minutes. Add the mushrooms and stir over a high heat for a few minutes until the mushrooms are cooked and the liquid has reduced (there should be about 2 tablespoons left). Season with salt and pepper, add the cream and pesto, and stir to mix.

3 Drain the pasta and add to the mushroom mixture in the pan. Check the seasoning. At the last moment, stir in the rocket leaves and allow to wilt for about 2 minutes. Serve immediately, scattered with Parmesan.

NOTE: The warm, peppery, pungent taste of rocket is one people love or hate. If you love it and you're making your own pesto for this dish, try substituting rocket for basil in the pesto recipe left.

Illustrated on page 177.

SPAGHETTI ALLA CARBONARA

SERVES 4

500g (1lb) spaghetti
salt and black pepper
175g (6oz) diced pancetta or streaky
   bacon, any rinds removed
1 garlic clove, crushed
4 eggs
125g (4oz) Parmesan cheese, grated
150ml (¼ pint) single cream
chopped parsley to garnish

1 Cook the spaghetti in a large saucepan of boiling salted water according to packet instructions.

2 Meanwhile, put the pancetta or bacon into a frying pan and heat gently for a few minutes until the fat runs. Increase the heat and add the garlic. Cook for 2–3 minutes or until the bacon is crisp.

3 Break the eggs into a bowl. Add the bacon and garlic mixture, using a slotted spoon. Add the Parmesan cheese, season generously with salt and pepper, and whisk until well blended.

4 Drain the spaghetti and return to the hot pan. Stir in the bacon and egg mixture and toss quickly until the egg just begins to set. Stir in the cream and heat gently. Serve at once, sprinkled with parsley.

Cook's know-how

It is best to buy a whole piece of Parmesan cheese and grate the quantity you need for a given dish. Ready grated Parmesan in packets is less economical and lacks the flavour of freshly grated Parmesan.

Spaghetti Alfredo

Heat 150ml (¼ pint) double cream with 30g (1oz) butter until the mixture has thickened. Set aside. Cook the pasta, drain, then add to the cream mixture. Add 90ml (3fl oz) more cream, 90g (3oz) Parmesan cheese, a pinch of grated nutmeg, and season with salt and pepper. Heat gently until thickened, and serve.

SPAGHETTI BOLOGNESE

SERVES 4

3tbsp olive oil
500g (1lb) minced beef
1 large onion, finely chopped
2 celery stalks, sliced
1tbsp plain flour
2 garlic cloves, crushed
90g (3oz) tomato purée
150ml (¼ pint) beef stock
150ml (¼ pint) red wine
1 x 400g (14oz) can chopped tomatoes
1tbsp redcurrant jelly
salt and black pepper
500g (1lb) spaghetti
grated Parmesan cheese to serve

1 Heat 2tbsp of the oil in a saucepan. Add the minced beef, onion, and celery, and cook, stirring, for 5 minutes or until the beef is browned. Add the flour, garlic, and tomato purée, and cook, stirring, for about 1 minute.

2 Pour in the stock and wine. Add the tomatoes and redcurrant jelly, season with salt and pepper, and bring to a boil. Cook, stirring, until the mixture has thickened.

3 Lower the heat, partially cover the pan, and simmer very gently, stirring occasionally, for about 1 hour.

4 Meanwhile, cook the spaghetti in boiling salted water according to packet instructions.

5 Return the spaghetti to the saucepan, add the remaining oil, and toss gently to coat.

6 Divide the spaghetti among warmed serving plates and ladle some of the sauce on top of each serving. Sprinkle with a little Parmesan cheese and hand the remainder separately.

CLASSIC LASAGNE

SERVES 8

125g (4oz) mature Cheddar cheese, grated
30g (1oz) Parmesan cheese, grated
175g (6oz) pre-cooked lasagne sheets
chopped fresh parsley to garnish

MEAT SAUCE

2tbsp olive oil
1kg (2lb) minced beef
45g (1½oz) plain flour
300ml (½ pint) beef stock
1 x 400g (14oz) can chopped tomatoes
6 celery stalks, finely sliced
2 onions, finely chopped
2 large garlic cloves, crushed
4tbsp tomato purée
1tsp sugar
salt and black pepper

WHITE SAUCE

60g (2oz) butter
45g (1½ oz) plain flour
600ml (1 pint) milk
1tsp Dijon mustard
¼tsp grated nutmeg

1 Make the meat sauce: heat the oil in a saucepan, add the beef, and cook, stirring, until browned.

2 Sprinkle in the flour and stir for 1 minute, then add the stock, tomatoes, celery, onions, garlic, tomato purée, and sugar. Season with salt and pepper and bring to a boil. Cover and simmer for 1 hour.

3 Meanwhile, make the white sauce: melt the butter in a saucepan, sprinkle in the flour and cook, stirring, for 1 minute. Remove from the heat and gradually blend in the milk. Bring to a boil, stirring until the mixture thickens. Simmer for 2–3 minutes. Stir in the mustard and nutmeg, and season with salt and pepper.

4 Spoon one-third of the meat sauce into a large shallow ovenproof dish, cover with one-third of the white sauce, and one-third of the Cheddar and Parmesan cheeses. Arrange half of the lasagne in a single layer. Repeat the layers, finishing with the Cheddar and Parmesan cheeses.

5 Bake in a preheated oven at 190°C (375°F, Gas 5) for 45–60 minutes until the pasta is tender and the topping is a golden brown colour. Serve at once, sprinkled with parsley.

SPAGHETTI ALL' AMATRICIANA

SERVES 6

1 red pepper
1 green pepper
4tbsp olive oil
5 unsmoked bacon or pancetta rashers, any rinds removed, diced
½–1 fresh green chilli, halved, seeded, and thinly sliced
3 garlic cloves, crushed
2 ripe tomatoes, finely chopped
2tbsp chopped flat-leaf parsley
salt and black pepper
500g (1lb) spaghetti
shavings of Parmesan cheese to serve

A speciality of Amatrice, near Rome, this tomato-based sauce is spiked with chilli and garlic, and richly flavoured with diced bacon and roast peppers.

1 Halve the red and green peppers, and remove the cores and seeds. Roast and peel the peppers. Cut the flesh into thin strips.

2 Heat the oil in a frying pan, add the bacon, and cook over a high heat for 5 minutes or until crisp. Add the roasted pepper strips and the chilli, and cook for 2 minutes. Stir in the garlic and cook for about 1 minute.

3 Add the tomatoes and parsley and cook for 3 minutes or until thickened. Remove from the heat and season with salt and pepper.

4 Cook the spaghetti in a large saucepan of boiling salted water according to packet instructions.

5 Drain the spaghetti thoroughly. Add the sauce and toss with the spaghetti. Serve at once, topped with Parmesan cheese shavings.

Spaghetti all' arrabbiata

Melt 30g (1oz) butter with 2tbsp olive oil in a frying pan, add 3 crushed garlic cloves and ½–1tsp crushed dried red chillies (chilli flakes), and cook gently. Drain 1 x 400g (14oz) can chopped tomatoes, stir the tomatoes into the pan, and bring slowly to a boil. Simmer until reduced and thickened, add ¼tsp dried oregano, and season with salt and black pepper. Toss with the spaghetti, and serve at once.

TUNA & FENNEL PASTA BAKE

SERVES 6

250g (8oz) pasta shells (conchiglie)
salt and black pepper
1tbsp sunflower oil
1 fennel bulb, trimmed and finely sliced
1 onion, finely sliced
60g (2oz) butter
60g (2oz) plain flour
600ml (1 pint) milk
1 x 200g (7oz) can tuna in brine,
    drained and flaked
3 hard-boiled eggs, coarsely chopped
125g (4oz) mature Cheddar
    cheese, grated
2tbsp chopped parsley to garnish

1 Cook the pasta shells in boiling salted water according to packet instructions until just tender. Drain thoroughly and set aside.

2 Heat the sunflower oil in a large frying pan, add the fennel and onion, and cook for 3–5 minutes until softened but not coloured. Set aside.

3 Melt the butter in a large saucepan, sprinkle in the flour, and cook, stirring, for 1 minute. Remove from the heat and gradually blend in the milk. Bring to a boil, stirring until the mixture thickens. Simmer for 2–3 minutes.

4 Stir in the cooked pasta, the fennel and onion, tuna, eggs, and cheese. Season with salt and pepper, then turn the mixture into a shallow ovenproof dish.

5 Bake in a preheated oven at 200°C (400°F, Gas 6) for about 30 minutes or until heated through and golden brown on top. Serve hot, sprinkled with chopped parsley.

Healthy option

To reduce fat, boil the fennel and onion with the pasta, make half the quantity of sauce in step 3, and make up the volume with pasta cooking water. You could also omit the eggs and halve the amount of cheese.

NASI GORENG

The name of this Indonesian recipe simply means fried rice. Prepared with a variety of ingredients, it is one of the best known Indonesian dishes, and one of the easiest to make. Traditional garnishes such as crushed peanuts, fried eggs and omelette strips give contrasting flavours and textures to the dish.

SERVES 6

375g (12oz) long grain rice
salt and black pepper
90ml (3fl oz) olive oil
6 streaky bacon rashers, chopped
2 large onions, chopped
3 garlic cloves, crushed
¼tsp chilli powder
2tsp mild curry powder
2 cooked chicken breasts, skinned
    and cut into small cubes
90ml (3fl oz) soy sauce
6 spring onions, chopped
60g (2oz) cooked peeled prawns
60g (2oz) almonds, halved, and toasted

TO GARNISH

coriander sprigs
6 fried eggs (optional)
prawn crackers

CHICKEN NASI GORENG

1 Cook the rice in boiling salted water for 12–15 minutes until tender. Drain, rinse with boiling water, drain again, and set aside.

2 Heat 1tbsp of the oil in a large frying pan or wok, add the bacon, and cook for 3–5 minutes until browned. Add the remaining oil, the onions, and garlic, and cook over a gentle heat for 3–5 minutes until the onions are soft but not coloured.

3 Add the chilli and curry powders and cook, stirring, for 1 minute or until fragrant. Add the chicken and cook for 5–6 minutes until just beginning to brown.

4 Add the soy sauce and half of the rice and stir well. Add the remaining rice, and season with salt and pepper. Cook over a gentle heat, stirring, for 7–8 minutes until the rice is heated through. Stir in the spring onions, prawns, and almonds, and heat through.

5 Serve hot, garnished with coriander sprigs, and fried eggs if you like. Serve prawn crackers in a separate bowl.

clockwise from top: *Chicken Nasi Goreng, Vegetarian Nasi Goreng, Quick Nasi Goreng.*

VEGETARIAN NASI GORENG

SERVES 6

375g (12oz) long grain rice
salt
2tbsp tamarind paste (optional)
2tbsp vegetable oil
1 red pepper, halved, seeded, and
  thinly sliced
1 large onion, chopped
3 garlic cloves, crushed
1cm (½in) piece of fresh root ginger,
  peeled and grated
2tsp curry powder
¼tsp each crushed dried red chillies
  (chilli flakes) and turmeric
½ small hard white cabbage,
  very thinly sliced
1 x 200g (7oz) can chopped tomatoes
3tbsp soy sauce

TO GARNISH

3 tomatoes, cut into strips
½ cucumber, cut into strips
omelette strips (see right)

1 Cook the rice in boiling salted water for 12–15 minutes until tender. Drain, rinse with boiling water, and drain again. Stir in the tamarind paste (if using) and set aside.

2 Heat 1tbsp of the oil in a large frying pan or wok, add the red pepper and onion, and cook for 3–5 minutes until softened. Add the garlic, ginger, curry powder, crushed chillies, and turmeric, and cook gently, stirring, for 1 minute.

3 Add the cabbage and cook for 3–5 minutes. Add the tomatoes and cook for 2–3 minutes. Remove from the pan.

4 Heat the remaining oil in the pan, add the rice, and cook gently until lightly browned. Return the vegetables to the pan. Add the soy sauce and heat gently to warm through.

5 Serve hot, garnished with tomato, cucumber, and omelette strips.

Illustrated on page 189.

QUICK NASI GORENG

SERVES 6

375g (12oz) long grain rice
2tbsp vegetable oil
1 onion, chopped
½tsp paprika
1tsp ground ginger
125g (4oz) button mushrooms, sliced
60g (2oz) bean sprouts
1tsp soy sauce
125g (4oz) cooked peeled prawns
2 spring onions, finely sliced
chopped coriander to garnish

1 Cook the rice in boiling salted water, for 12–15 minutes until tender. Drain, rinse with boiling water, drain again, and set aside.

2 Heat 1tbsp of the oil in a frying pan or wok, add the onion, and cook for 3–5 minutes until soft. Add the paprika and ginger, and cook over a low heat for 1 minute. Add the mushrooms and bean sprouts and cook for 2–3 minutes until softened. Remove from the pan.

3 Heat the remaining oil in the pan, add the rice, and cook over a gentle heat, stirring, for 7–8 minutes to warm through. Stir in the soy sauce. Return the vegetables to the pan and add the prawns and onions. Serve hot, garnished with coriander.

Illustrated on page 189.

Illustrated on page 189.

Omelette garnish

Whisk 2 eggs with plenty of salt and pepper. Melt 30g (1oz) butter in an omelette pan or small frying pan. Add the eggs to the pan and cook until set. Slide the omelette out of the pan and roll it up, then leave to cool before slicing across into fine strips.

STIR-FRIED CHINESE NOODLES

SERVES 4

5 dried shiitake mushrooms
250ml (8fl oz) hot vegetable stock
375g (12oz) Chinese egg noodles
salt
about 2tsp soy sauce
1tbsp sunflower oil
250g (8oz) mangetout
3 garlic cloves, crushed
5mm (¼in) piece of fresh root
    ginger, peeled and grated
¼tsp sugar
125g (4oz) bean sprouts
about ½tsp crushed dried red
    chillies (chilli flakes)

TO SERVE

3 spring onions, sliced
2tsp sesame oil
1tbsp chopped fresh coriander

1 Put the mushrooms into a bowl, pour over the hot vegetable stock, and leave to soak for about 30 minutes.

2 Drain the mushrooms, reserving the liquid. Squeeze the mushrooms dry, then cut into thin strips.

3 Cook the noodles in a large saucepan of boiling salted water for 3 minutes or according to packet instructions. Drain the noodles, toss with soy sauce to taste, and set aside.

4 Heat the sunflower oil in a wok or large frying pan, add the mushrooms, mangetout, garlic, and ginger, and stir-fry for 2 minutes. Add the sugar, bean sprouts, crushed chillies to taste, and 3tbsp of the reserved mushroom soaking liquid. Stir-fry for 2 minutes.

5 Add the egg noodles and stir-fry for 2 minutes or until heated through. Serve at once, sprinkled with the spring onions, sesame oil, and coriander.

RISOTTO AL VERDE

SERVES 6

15g (½oz) butter
3 garlic cloves, crushed
250g (8oz) risotto rice
1 litre (1¾ pints) hot vegetable stock
175ml (6fl oz) single cream
90g (3oz) blue cheese, crumbled
4tbsp ready made pesto (see page 179)
90g (3oz) Parmesan cheese, grated
4tbsp pine nuts, lightly toasted
4tbsp shredded fresh basil

1 Melt the butter in a large saucepan. When it is foaming, add the garlic and cook gently for 1 minute.

2 Add the risotto rice, stirring to coat the grains in the butter, and cook for 2 minutes. Add a ladleful of the hot vegetable stock, and cook gently, stirring constantly, until the stock has been absorbed. Continue to add the stock, a ladleful at a time, and cook for 20–25 minutes or until the rice is just tender.

3 Add the cream, and cook gently, stirring, until it has been absorbed. Stir in the blue cheese, then the pesto, Parmesan, and pine nuts. Garnish with shredded fresh basil, and serve.

Chicken & mushroom risotto

Add 125g (4oz) sliced mushrooms to the saucepan with the garlic in step 1 and cook for 3–5 minutes until the mushrooms are soft. Substitute chicken stock for the vegetable stock, omit the blue cheese and pesto, then add 250g (8oz) cooked diced chicken with the cream in step 3.

Asparagus risotto

Add 1 finely chopped onion to the pan with the garlic in step 1, and cook for 3–5 minutes until soft. Omit the blue cheese and pesto, and add 375g (12oz) trimmed and chopped asparagus in step 2, about 5 minutes before the end of the cooking time.

Vegetables & Salads

GLAZED CARROTS & TURNIPS

SERVES 4

375g (12oz) carrots, cut into 5cm (2in) strips
375g (12oz) baby turnips
300ml (½ pint) chicken stock
30g (1oz) butter
1tsp caster sugar
salt and black pepper
1tbsp mixed chopped fresh mint and parsley

1 Put the vegetables into a pan with the stock, butter, and sugar. Season with salt and pepper, and bring to a boil. Cover and cook for about 10 minutes until the vegetables are almost tender.

2 Remove the lid and boil rapidly until the liquid in the pan has evaporated and formed a glaze on the vegetables. Stir in the herbs, and serve hot.

SUMMER PEAS & BEANS

SERVES 6–8

250g (8oz) shelled fresh broad beans
  (they must be young)
salt and black pepper
250g (8oz) shelled peas
  (they must be young)
250g (8oz) French beans, halved
30g (1oz) butter
2tbsp chopped fresh mint
fresh mint to garnish

1 Cook the broad beans in a saucepan of boiling salted water for a few minutes until just tender. Add the peas and French beans and cook for another 5–10 minutes or until tender (the timing depends on their freshness).

2 Drain all the vegetables, and return to the pan. Add the butter and mint, and stir until the butter melts. Taste for seasoning, and serve hot, garnished with fresh mint.

CHARGRILLED VEGETABLE PLATTER

SERVES 6

1 small aubergine
salt and black pepper
1 small courgette
1 red pepper
1 yellow pepper
1 large red onion
500g (1lb) asparagus
4 large mushrooms
175g (6oz) pattypan squash
olive oil for brushing
8–10 wooden cocktail sticks

1 Prepare the vegetables. Trim the aubergine, cut in half lengthwise, and score a criss-cross pattern on the cut surfaces.

2 Cut the courgette in half lengthwise. Cut the red peppers in half lengthwise, and cut out the fleshy ribs and seeds. Peel the red onioin and cut lengthwise into 4–6 wedges. Trim the woody ends from the asparagus and cut the spears to an even length.

3 Gently wipe the mushrooms with damp paper towels and remove the stalks. Trim the squash, if necessary.

4 Place the asparagus spears side by side in groups of 3 or 4 (depending on thickness). Gently push a cocktail stick through the asparagus, about 1cm (½in) from the tips, until they are all skewered. Insert a second cocktail stick at the bases of the spears. Repeat for the remaining groups of asparagus spears.

5 Brush all of the vegetables generously with olive oil, and season with salt and pepper to taste.

6 Place a batch at a time over a hot barbecue or on a preheated ridged griddle pan, and cook for 10–15 minutes, turning occasionally, until the vegtables are lightly charred. Keep each batch warm while you cook the remaining vegetables.

Cook's know-how

If you are using a ridged chargrill pan, either non-stick or cast iron, it is important to preheat it empty first, before laying the food on the ridges. Never oil the pan before preheating, as this will cause it to smoke. The secret is to oil the food, not the pan, and put the food in once the pan is good and hot. Press down hard on the food to help mark the ridges, and avoid moving the food in the pan as this will prevent the ridges from charring.

MIXED LEAF SALAD

SERVES 4–6

1 crisp lettuce, such as iceberg
  or romaine
1 bunch of watercress, tough
  stalks removed
60g (2oz) lamb's lettuce
60g (2oz) rocket
about 4tbsp vinaigrette dressing
1tbsp snipped fresh chives

1 Tear the lettuce leaves into bite-sized pieces and put them into a large salad bowl. Add the watercress, lamb's lettuce, and rocket, and mix together.

2 Pour the dressing over the salad and toss gently. Sprinkle with the chives, and serve at once.

Cook's know-how

When making a leafy salad, do not drown the leaves in dressing – there should be just enough to cling to the leaves. Add the dressing just before serving so the leaves stay crisp, and toss gently until each leaf is lightly and evenly coated.

VINAIGRETTE DRESSING

Put 6tbsp olive oil, 2tbsp white wine vinegar, 1tbsp lemon juice, 1tbsp Dijon mustard, 1tsp caster sugar, and salt and pepper to taste into a screw-topped jar. Shake until combined. This makes 150ml (¼ pint).

SERVES 4–6

1 cucumber, peeled and cut
  in half lengthwise
1tbsp chopped fresh dill

DRESSING

2tbsp hot water
2tbsp white wine vinegar
1tbsp sunflower oil
2tbsp caster sugar
salt and black pepper

CUCUMBER SALAD

1 Scoop out the cucumber seeds. Cut the flesh crosswise into thin slices, and arrange in a serving dish.

2 Make the dressing: whisk together the water, wine vinegar, oil, sugar, and salt and pepper to taste.

3 Pour the dressing over the cucumber and sprinkle with the dill before serving.

Serving suggestion

This Danish-style salad goes well with both grilled or baked fresh fish and smoked fish.

TOMATO & ONION SALAD

SERVES 6

750g (1½lb) ripe but firm tomatoes, thinly sliced
1 mild onion, cut into thin rings
1tbsp snipped fresh chives

DRESSING

90ml (3fl oz) extra virgin olive oil
2tbsp red wine vinegar
1tsp caster sugar
salt and black pepper

1 Overlap the tomato slices in circles of diminishing size in a large shallow dish. Arrange the onion rings on top.

2 Make the dressing: combine the olive oil, red wine vinegar, and caster sugar, and add salt and pepper to taste.

3 Spoon the dressing over the tomatoes and onions, cover, and leave to chill for about 2 hours. Sprinkle with the snipped chives before serving.

TOMATO & BASIL SALAD

SERVES 4–6

2 beefsteak or slicing tomatoes
4 ripe salad tomatoes
125g (4oz) cherry tomatoes
1 yellow pepper, cored, deseeded,
   and cut into chunks
2tbsp shredded fresh basil

DRESSING

3tbsp extra virgin olive oil
2tsp balsamic vinegar
1tsp caster sugar
salt and black pepper

1 Make the dressing: combine the olive oil, vinegar, sugar, and salt and pepper to taste.

2 Cut the tomatoes in half lengthwise, cut out the core, and cut each half into 4 wedges. Thickly slice the salad tomatoes. Halve the cherry tomatoes.

3 Put all the tomatoes and the yellow pepper into a salad bowl, and sprinkle with the dressing. Cover and leave to stand for 1 hour to let the flavours mingle. Sprinkle with the basil just before serving.

GRATIN DAUPHINOIS

SERVES 8

butter for greasing
150ml (¼ pint) single cream
150ml (¼ pint) double cream
1 large garlic clove, crushed
1kg (2lb) main-crop potatoes
salt and black pepper
125g (4oz) Gruyère cheese, grated

1 Lightly butter a shallow gratin dish. Put the single and double creams into a bowl, add the garlic, and stir to mix.

2 Thinly slice the potatoes, preferably with the slicing disc of a food processor.

3 Prepare the gratin dauphinois (see box, below).

4 Bake in a preheated oven at 160°C (325°F, Gas 3) for 1½ hours or until the potatoes are tender, and the topping is golden brown. Serve at once.

PREPARING THE GRATIN DAUPHINOIS

Arrange a layer of potatoes, slightly overlapping, in the bottom of the gratin dish. Season with salt and pepper.

Pour a little of the cream mixture over the potatoes, then sprinkle with grated cheese. Continue layering the potatoes, cream, and cheese, and adding salt and pepper, then finish with a layer of cheese.

GARLIC CREAMED POTATOES

SERVES 4

750g (1½lb) floury potatoes, cut into
   large chunks
4 garlic cloves, unpeeled
salt and black pepper
1 x 200g carton créme fraîche
30g (1oz) butter
2tbsp snipped fresh chives

1 Cook the potatoes and whole garlic cloves in boiling salted water for 20–30 minutes until tender. Drain thoroughly, and peel the skins off the garlic cloves.

2 Return the potatoes to the saucepan and toss over a gentle heat for a few seconds to dry thoroughly, shaking the saucepan so that the potatoes do not burn.

3 Mash the potatoes and garlic together, or work through a sieve for a finer purée, then push them to one side of the pan.

4 Add the créme fraîche to the saucepan and heat until very hot. Beat the cream into the potatoes and garlic with the butter, and salt and pepper to taste. Sprinkle with chives, and serve hot.

Herb & cheese creamed potatoes

Omit the garlic, and add 2tbsp chopped fresh parsley and 60g (2oz) finely grated Cheddar cheese when you beat in the cream.

Creamed potatoes with swede

Omit the garlic and fresh chives. Substitute 250g (8oz) swede, cut into small chunks, for 250g (8oz) of the potatoes, and add a pinch of grated nutmeg just before serving.

CRUNCHY ORIENTAL SALAD

SERVES 6

1 iceberg or romaine lettuce
175g (6oz) bean sprouts
6 spring onions, thinly sliced on
 the diagonal
1 green pepper, halved, seeded,
 and thinly sliced
2tbsp toasted sesame seeds

DRESSING

3tbsp sunflower or olive oil
1tsp sesame oil
1tbsp white wine vinegar
1 garlic clove, crushed
1cm (½in) piece of fresh root ginger,
 peeled and grated
½tsp caster sugar, or to taste
salt and black pepper

1 Tear the lettuce leaves into bite-sized pieces. Put the lettuce, bean sprouts, spring onions, and pepper into a salad bowl and mix together.

2 Make the dressing: combine the oils, vinegar, garlic, and ginger, and season to taste with sugar, salt, and pepper. Whisk until smooth.

3 Toss the salad with the dressing, sprinkle with the sesame seeds, and serve.

SERVES 4–6

4 beefsteak or slicing tomatoes
1 cucumber, sliced
250g (8oz) feta cheese, diced
24 black olives, pitted
125ml (4fl oz) extra virgin olive oil
4tbsp lemon juice
salt and black pepper
2tbsp chopped fresh mint or
   flat-leaf parsley

GREEK SALAD

1 Halve the tomatoes lengthwise, cut out the cores, and cut each half into 4 wedges.

2 Put the tomatoes into a large salad bowl, and add the cucumber, feta cheese, and olives.

3 Spoon over the olive oil and lemon juice, and add salt and black pepper to taste (do not use too much salt as feta is a salty cheese), then toss gently to mix.

4 Sprinkle the salad with the mint or parsley before serving.

SERVES 4

250g (8oz) French beans, cut in
  half crosswise
salt and black pepper
1 x 400g (13oz) can chick peas,
  drained and rinsed
1 x 400g (13oz) can red kidney beans,
  drained and rinsed
10 pitted black olives, halved
chopped parsley to garnish

DRESSING

4tbsp Greek yogurt
3tbsp olive oil
3tbsp red wine vinegar
2tsp Dijon mustard
¼tsp caster sugar, or to taste

THREE-BEAN SALAD

1 Cook the French beans in boiling salted water for 4–5 minutes until just tender. Drain, rinse under cold running water, and drain again.

2 Make the dressing: combine the Greek yogurt, oil, red wine vinegar, and mustard, and season with sugar, salt, and pepper to taste, and whisk until smooth.

3 Put the chick peas, red kidney beans, and French beans into a large bowl. Pour the dressing over the beans and stir gently to mix. Cover and leave to stand for 1 hour. Add the olives, sprinkle with the chopped parsley, and serve at once.

Three-bean salad with bacon

Substitute 250g (8oz) shelled and skinned broad beans for the chick peas, and omit the olives. Cut 60g (2oz) streaky bacon rashers into strips, and dry-fry until crisp and golden. Sprinkle over the salad just before serving.

AVOCADO SALAD

SERVES 6

60g (2oz) pine nuts
250g (8oz) mixed salad leaves
2 oranges
2 avocados

DRESSING

finely grated zest of 1 orange
3tbsp orange juice
1tbsp walnut oil
1–2tsp caster sugar
salt and black pepper

1 Spread the pine nuts on a baking tray, and toast under a hot grill for 2 minutes until golden brown, watching carefully.

2 Put the salad leaves into a large salad bowl. Peel the oranges, removing the rind and pith, and separate into segments.

3 Halve, stone, and peel the avocados. Slice lengthwise and mix with the orange segments and pine nuts.

4 Whisk together the dressing ingredients, and pour over the salad. Toss gently and serve.

AUBERGINE WITH FRESH PESTO

SERVES 4

1 large aubergine
75ml (2½fl oz) olive oil, plus
   extra for greasing
2–3tsp balsamic or wine vinegar
fresh pesto (see box, below)
shredded fresh basil to garnish

1 Cut the aubergine crosswise into thin slices and arrange in a single layer on a lightly oiled baking tray. Brush the slices with one-quarter of the oil, place under a hot grill, 7cm (3in) from the heat, and grill for 5 minutes or until lightly browned. Turn, brush with one-third of the remaining oil, and grill 5 minutes more.

2 Sprinkle the remaining oil and the vinegar over the aubergine slices. Leave to cool. Spread pesto over one side of each slice, garnish with fresh basil, and serve at room temperature.

Cook's know-how

Keep fresh pesto in jar in the fridge for up to 1 week or freeze for up to 1 month.

FRESH PESTO

Purée 60g (2oz) grated Parmesan cheese, 1 garlic clove, 60g (2oz) pine nuts, 60g (2oz) fresh basil leaves, and salt and pepper to taste in a food processor until almost smooth.

Add 75ml (2½fl oz) olive oil gradually, with the blades turning, scraping the side of the bowl with a rubber spatula to ensure that all the mixture is incorporated.

Pies, Tarts, and Hot Puddings

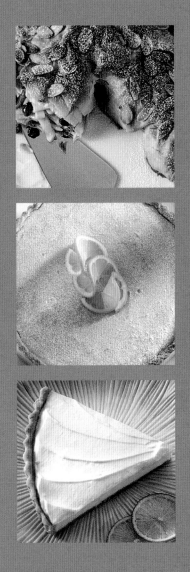

TREACLE PUDDING

SERVES 4–6

butter for greasing
6 generous tbsp golden syrup
125g (4oz) self-raising flour
125g (4oz) shredded vegetable
  suet or grated chilled butter
125g (4oz) fresh white breadcrumbs
60g (2oz) caster sugar
about 125ml (4fl oz) milk
900ml (1½ pint) pudding bowl

1 Lightly butter the bowl and spoon the golden syrup into the bottom.

2 Put the flour, suet or butter, breadcrumbs, and sugar into a bowl and stir to combine. Stir in enough milk to give a dropping consistency. Spoon into the bowl on top of the syrup.

3 Cover the bowl with buttered foil, pleated in the middle. Secure by tying string under the rim of the bowl.

4 Put the bowl into a steamer or saucepan of simmering water, making sure the water comes halfway up the side of the bowl if using a saucepan. Cover and steam, topping up with boiling water as needed, for about 3 hours. Turn out the pudding, and serve.

BREAD & BUTTER PUDDING

SERVES 6

12 thin slices of white bread,
   crusts removed
about 125g (4oz) butter, softened,
   plus extra for greasing
175g (6oz) mixed dried fruit
grated zest of 2 lemons
125g (4oz) demerara sugar
600ml (1 pint) full cream milk
2 eggs
1.7 litre (3 pint) ovenproof dish

1 Spread one side of each slice of bread with a thick layer of butter. Cut each slice of bread in half, diagonally. Lightly butter the ovenproof dish and arrange 12 of the triangles, buttered-side down, in the bottom of the dish.

2 Sprinkle over half of the dried fruit, lemon zest, and sugar. Top with the remaining bread, buttered-side up. Sprinkle over the remaining fruit, lemon zest, and sugar.

3 Beat together the milk and eggs, and strain over the bread. Leave for 1 hour so that the bread can absorb some of the liquid.

4 Bake in a preheated oven at 180°C (350°F, Gas 4) for about 40 minutes until the bread slices on the top of the pudding are a golden brown colour and crisp, and the custard mixture has set completely. Serve at once.

Cook's know-how

To enrich the pudding, add half milk and half single cream.

Bread & butter pudding with marmalade

Spread 6 of the slices of bread with thick-cut marmalade after spreading all of them with the butter. Halve the slices, and arrange the buttered ones buttered-side down in the dish. Sprinkle with the dried fruit, lemon zest, and sugar, then arrange the remaining triangles, marmalade-side up, on top.

TARTE AU CITRON

SERVES 10–12

9 eggs
300ml (½ pint) double cream
grated zest and juice of 5 large lemons
375g (12oz) caster sugar
icing sugar for dusting
lemon twists to decorate

PASTRY

250g (8oz) plain flour
125g (4oz) chilled butter,
   cut into cubes
60g (2oz) caster sugar
1 egg
2tbsp water
28cm (11in) 4cm (1½in) deep
   loose-bottomed fluted
   flan tin
baking beans

1 Make the pastry: put the flour into a large bowl. Add the butter and rub in with the fingertips until the mixture resembles fine breadcrumbs.

2 Stir in caster sugar, then bind together with egg and water to make a soft, pliable dough. Wrap in cling film and chill for 30 minutes.

3 Roll out the dough on a lightly floured surface and use to line the flan tin. Bake blind in a preheated oven at 200°C (400°F, Gas 6) for 10 minutes.

4 Remove the baking beans and foil, and bake the pastry shell for 5 minutes or until the base has dried out. Remove from the oven and reduce the oven temperature to 180°C (350°F, Gas 4).

5 Beat the eggs in a bowl and add the cream, lemon zest and juice, and caster sugar. Stir until smooth, and pour into the pastry shell.

6 Bake for 35–40 minutes until the lemon filling has set. Cover the tart loosely with foil if the pastry begins to brown too much.

7 Leave the tart to cool a little, then dust with icing sugar. Decorate with lemon twists, and serve warm or at room temperature.

APPLE STRUDEL

SERVES 8

four 25 x 45cm (10 x 18in) sheets
of filo pastry
60g (2oz) butter, melted
30g (1oz) fresh white breadcrumbs
15g (½oz) flaked almonds
icing sugar for dusting

FILLING

750g (1½lb) cooking apples, quartered,
cored, peeled, and sliced
grated zest and juice of 1 lemon
3tbsp light muscovado sugar
½tsp ground mixed spice
½tsp ground cinnamon
125g (4oz) sultanas
60g (2oz) blanched almonds,
roughly chopped

1 Make the filling: mix together the apples, lemon zest and juice, sugar, mixed spice, cinnamon, sultanas, and almonds.

2 Lightly brush 1 sheet of filo pastry with melted butter. Cover with the remaining sheets, brushing each with butter. Add the filling and finish the strudel (see box, below).

3 Brush the strudel with melted butter and sprinkle the almonds. Bake in a preheated oven at 190°C (375°F, Gas 5) for 40–45 minutes until the pastry is crisp and golden. Dust with icing sugar. Serve warm or cold.

FINISHING THE STRUDEL

Sprinkle the breadcrumbs over the pastry. Spoon the apple mixture along the middle of the pastry.

Fold the pastry to enclose the filling, turn over on to a baking tray, and bend into a horseshoe shape.

KEY LIME PIE

SERVES 8

300ml (½ pint) double cream
1 x 400g (13oz) can sweetened
   condensed milk
grated zest and juice of 1 lime
lime slices to decorate

PASTRY

175g (6oz) plain flour
90g (3oz) chilled butter, cut into
   cubes
about 2tbsp cold water
23cm (9in) loose-bottomed fluted
   flan tin
baking beans

1 Make the pastry: put the flour into a large bowl, add the butter, and rub in until the mixture resembles fine breadcrumbs. Add enough cold water to make a soft pliable dough.

2 Wrap the dough in cling film or foil and chill in the refrigerator for 30 minutes.

3 Roll out the dough on a lightly floured surface and use to line the flan tin.

4 Bake the pastry shell blind in a preheated oven at 200°C (400°F, Gas 6) for about 10 minutes. Remove the baking beans and foil, and return the shell to the oven for 5 minutes. Cool slightly.

5 Whip the cream to soft peaks in a large bowl and mix together with the condensed milk. Slowly stir in the lime zest and juice until the mixture thickens.

6 Pour the mixture into the shell and smooth the top, or create a pattern with a palette knife. Chill in the refrigerator for at least 2 hours or until the filling is set firm.

7 Serve the pie chilled, decorated with lime slices.

QUEEN OF PUDDINGS

SERVES 6

4 egg yolks
600ml (1 pint) milk
30g (1oz) butter, plus extra
   for greasing
60g (2oz) caster sugar
grated zest of 1 orange
90g (3oz) fresh white breadcrumbs
3tbsp strawberry or raspberry jam

MERINGUE TOPPING

4 egg whites
175g (6oz) caster sugar
shallow 1.25 litre (2 pint)
ovenproof dish

1 In a large bowl, lightly beat the egg yolks. Set aside. Heat the milk in a small saucepan until bubbles appear around the edge. Add the butter, sugar, and orange zest, and heat gently until the butter has melted and the sugar dissolved.

2 Lightly butter the ovenproof dish and set aside. Gradually add the hot milk mixture to the egg yolks, whisking all the time.

3 Stir in the breadcrumbs, then pour into the ovenproof dish. Leave to stand for 15 minutes.

4 Bake the pudding in a preheated oven at 180°C (350°F, Gas 4) for about 30 minutes until just set. Remove from the oven and set aside.

5 Warm the jam in a small saucepan until melted. Spread the warmed jam evenly over the surface of the set pudding.

6 Make the meringue topping: with an electric mixer, whisk the egg whites until stiff but not dry. Whisk in the caster sugar, 1tsp at a time, keeping the mixer at full speed.

7 Spoon the meringue on top of the pudding, spread it to the edge and pull it up to form peaks.

8 Return the pudding to the oven and bake for a further 10–15 minutes until the top of the meringue is crisp and golden brown. Serve at once.

Chilled Puddings

TIRAMISU

SERVES 8

1 heaped tsp instant coffee granules
125ml (4fl oz) boiling water
3tbsp brandy
2 eggs
65g (2½oz) caster sugar
250g (8oz) mascarpone cheese
300ml (½ pint) double cream,
  whipped until thick
8 trifle sponges
60g (2oz) plain dark chocolate,
  coarsely grated
30g (1oz) white chocolate,
  coarsely grated, to decorate

1 Dissolve the coffee in the measured boiling water and mix with the brandy.

2 Combine the eggs and caster sugar in a large bowl and whisk together until thick and light, and the mixture leaves a trail on the surface.

3 Put the mascarpone into a bowl and stir in a little of the egg mixture. Fold in the rest, then fold in the cream.

4 Cut the trifle sponges horizontally in half. Layer the tiramisu (see box, below) with half the sponges, pour over half the coffee and brandy mixture, spoon half the mascarpone mixture, and sprinkle half the plain chocolate.

5 Repeat the layers with the remaining ingredients, decorating the top with the grated white chocolate, and the remaining grated plain chocolate. Cover and chill for at least 4 hours before serving.

LAYERING THE TIRAMISU

Line the bottom of a large glass serving bowl with half of the sponge pieces. Drizzle half of the coffee and brandy mixture over the sponges.

SUMMER PUDDING

SERVES 6

8 slices of stale medium-sliced white
bread, crusts removed
875g (1¾lb) mixed summer fruits such
as strawberries, redcurrants,
blackcurrants, cherries,
and raspberries
150g (5oz) caster sugar
75ml (2½fl oz) water
2tbsp framboise or crème de
cassis liqueur
crème fraîche or Greek yogurt
to serve
1.25 litre (2 pint) pudding bowl

This classic English summer-time treat is very easy to
make, and not at all high in calories. For a perfect,
evenly coloured result, reserve half of the cooking
juices and pour them over any pale patches of bread
after unmoulding the pudding.

1 Set 2 slices of bread aside for the top of the
pudding, then use the remaining slices to line the
bowl (see box, left).

2 Hull and halve the strawberries if large, strip the
currants from their stalks, and pit the cherries.

3 Place the redcurrants, blackcurrants, and cherries
in a saucepan with the sugar and measured water. Heat
gently until the juices begin to run. Stir until the sugar
has dissolved, and cook until all of the fruit is just tender.

4 Remove from the heat and add the strawberries,
raspberries, and liqueur. Spoon the fruit and half of
the juice into the lined bowl, reserving the remaining
juice. Cover the top of the fruit with the reserved
bread slices.

5 Stand the bowl in a shallow dish to catch any
overflowing juices, then put a saucer on top of the
bread lid. Place a kitchen weight on top of the saucer.
Leave to chill for 8 hours.

6 Invert the pudding on to a serving plate. Spoon the
reserved juices over the top, paying attention to pale
areas. Serve with either crème fraîche or Greek yogurt.

LINING THE PUDDING BOWL

Put a slice of bread in the bottom of the bowl,
cutting it to fit if necessary, then use the
remainder to line the sides. The slices should
fit snugly together.

CARAMELIZED ORANGES

SERVES 4

250g (8oz) granulated sugar
150ml (¼ pint) cold water
150ml (¼ pint) lukewarm water
3tbsp orange liqueur
8 thin-skinned oranges

1 Put the sugar and measured cold water into a heavy pan and heat gently until the sugar dissolves.

2 When all the sugar has dissolved, bring to a boil and boil steadily until a rich brown colour. (If the caramel is too light in colour it will be very sweet, but be careful not to let it burn.)

3 Protect your hand by covering it with a cloth, and remove the pan from the heat. Pour the measured lukewarm water into the caramel.

4 Return the pan to the heat and stir to melt the caramel. Pour the caramel into a heatproof serving dish. Leave to cool for 30 minutes. Stir in the orange liqueur.

5 Pare the zest from 1 of the oranges, using a vegetable peeler. Cut the zest into very thin strips. Cook for 1 minute in boiling water, drain, rinse thoroughly under cold running water, and set aside.

6 Using a sharp knife, remove the peel and pith from each orange, catching any juice to add to the caramel in the dish. Cut each orange into slices crosswise, then reassemble the oranges, holding the slices together with cocktail sticks.

7 Place the oranges in the dish of caramel and spoon the caramel over them. Scatter the strips of orange zest over the top. Chill for about 30 minutes. Remove the cocktail sticks before transferring the oranges to individual bowls to serve.

LEMON SYLLABUB

SERVES 4

75ml (⅛ pint) dessert wine
or sweet white wine
If you do not have any sweet dessert
wine, use ordinary white wine and
increase the sugar by 25g (1oz)
2 large lemons
90g (3oz) caster sugar
300ml (½ pint) double cream

1 Put the wine into a bowl with the grated zest and juice of 1 of the lemons, and sugar. Stir to mix, then leave to stand for about 15 minutes, stirring occasionally, until the sugar has dissolved.

2 Meanwhile, remove the zest from the remaining lemon in long, very thin strips. Blanch the strips in a small saucepan of boiling water for 1 minute. Drain, rinse under cold running water, and pat dry.

3 In a medium bowl, whip the cream until it just holds its shape. Add the wine mixture very slowly, whisking well between each addition to ensure that the mixture remains thick.

4 Spoon into 4 tall syllabub glasses. Decorate the top of each syllabub with a strip of lemon zest, and serve at once.

Cook's know-how

For a less rich syllabub, use half whipped double cream and half Greek yogurt. Do not use whipping cream instead of double cream because it will not be heavy enough to hold the weight of the wine. Serve with shortbread biscuits, if you like.

PAVLOVA WITH PINEAPPLE & GINGER

SERVES 6–8

4 egg whites
250g (8oz) caster sugar
1½tsp cornflour
1½tsp white wine vinegar

TOPPING

375ml (13fl oz) double or
   whipping cream
60g (2oz) stem ginger in syrup,
   cut into matchstick-thin strips
1 x 400g (13oz) can pineapple
   rings, drained

Pavlova meringue is crisp on the outside, soft and slightly chewy like marshmallows inside. This pineapple and ginger topping is good in winter, but if you want to make a summer pavlova, use sweetened fresh red berries instead – and omit the ginger.

1 Preheat the oven to 160°C (325°F, Gas 3). Mark a 23cm (9in) circle on a sheet of non-stick baking parchment, turn the paper over, and line a baking tray.

2 Make the meringue: with an electric mixer, whisk the egg whites until stiff but not dry. Whisk in the caster sugar, 1tsp at a time, keeping the mixer at full speed. Blend the cornflour and vinegar and whisk into the egg white mixture.

3 Spread the mixture inside the circle on the baking parchment, building the sides up so that they are higher than the middle. Place in the oven, then immediately reduce the heat to 150°C (300°F, Gas 2).

4 Bake the meringue for 1½ hours or until firm to the touch. Leave the meringue inside for another hour. Peel the lining paper from the meringue, and transfer it to a serving plate. Leave to cool.

5 Before serving, whip the cream until stiff, and stir in half of the stem ginger strips. Spoon the mixture into the middle of the meringue. Top with the pineapple rings and the remaining stem ginger strips.

Cook's know-how

Keep the oven door closed when you leave the meringue to dry out, but if you have a fan-assisted oven, you should leave the door slightly open. The meringue base can be made a day in advance and kept in an airtight container in a cool place until needed. Add the cream and fruit topping just before serving.

STRAWBERRY MERINGUE ROULADE

SERVES 8

sunflower oil for greasing
4 egg whites
250g (8oz) caster sugar
45g (1½oz) flaked almonds
icing sugar for dusting

FILLING

300ml (½ pint) double or
  whipping cream, whipped
  until thick
250g (8oz) strawberries,
  quartered
23 x 33cm (9 x 13in) Swiss roll tin

1 Lightly oil the Swiss roll tin and line with a sheet of baking parchment.

2 Whisk the egg whites until stiff but not dry. Add the sugar, 1tsp at a time, and continue to whisk, until all the sugar has been incorporated and the mixture is stiff and glossy.

3 Spoon the meringue into the lined tin and tilt to level the surface. Sprinkle over the flaked almonds. Bake near the top of a preheated oven at 200°C (400°F, Gas 6) for about 8 minutes until the top is golden brown.

4 Reduce the oven temperature to 160°C (325°F, Gas 3), and continue baking for 10 minutes or until the meringue is firm to the touch.

5 Remove the meringue from the oven and turn out on to a sheet of baking parchment. Peel the lining paper from the base and leave the meringue to cool for 10 minutes.

6 Spread the whipped cream evenly over the meringue, and scatter the strawberries over the cream.

7 Roll up the meringue from a long side, using the lining paper to lift it. Wrap the roulade in baking parchment and leave to chill for about 30 minutes. Dust with sifted icing sugar before serving.

FRUIT SALADS

A fruit salad is welcome at the end of any meal any time of year, whether it is a simple family supper or a special occasion. All of these fruit salads can be made well in advance and served just as they are, or with cream or ice cream, crème fraîche, or yogurt.

SERVES 4–6

500g (1lb) mixed no-need-to-soak
   dried fruits, eg pears, peaches,
   mango, prunes, pineapple,
   figs, apples
about 900ml (1½ pints) apple juice
1 vanilla pod
75g (2½oz) dried cranberries
75g (2½oz) dried cherries

SPICED FRUIT SALAD

1 Put the mixed fruits into a saucepan with 900ml (1½ pints) apple juice and the vanilla pod. Bring to a boil and simmer gently for about 15 minutes.

2 Add the dried cranberries and cherries to the pan, and continue cooking for about 15 minutes, adding more apple juice (or water) if necessary. Serve hot or cold.

clockwise from top: *Spiced Fruit Salad, Orange Passion Salad, Tropical Island Fruit Salad, Fruits of the Forest Salad.*

TROPICAL ISLAND FRUIT SALAD

SERVES 6

1 small ripe pineapple
1 ripe charentais or cantaloupe melon
1 ripe mango
250g (8oz) seedless black grapes
150ml (¼ pint) pineapple and
  coconut juice or pineapple juice
125g (4oz) physalis
  (cape gooseberries)
2 Asian (nashi) pears

1 Cut the top and bottom off the pineapple. Remove the skin with a sharp knife, then cut out the brown eyes. Cut the pineapple lengthwise into 4 and remove and discard the hard inner core. Cut the flesh into chunks and put into a large glass serving bowl.

2 Cut the melon into quarters, remove and discard the seeds with a spoon. Cut each melon quarter in half, remove the skin with a sharp knife, and cut the flesh into chunks. Add to the pineapple.

3 Peel the mango, cut either side of the large flat stone which is in the middle of the mango, and cut the flesh into pieces. Add to the bowl with the grapes. Pour over the fruit juice, cover, and chill in the refrigerator for about 2 hours, or overnight.

4 Peel back the paper lanterns on the physalis. Remove the fruits from about half of the physalis, wipe gently with kitchen paper, and add to the bowl.

5 Peel and quarter the pears, remove the cores, and slice the flesh into the bowl.

6 Stir the fruits, making sure the pear is submerged in juice or it will discolour. Cover and chill in the refrigerator for about 1 hour. Serve chilled, decorated with the remaining physalis.

Illustrated on page 241.

SERVES 6–8

250g (8oz) fresh cranberries
60g (2oz) caster sugar
250g (8oz) strawberries, hulled
and halved if large
125g (4oz) blueberries
250g (8oz) raspberries
250g (8oz) blackberries
250g (8oz) loganberries, or increase
the amount of the other berries
if loganberries are unavailable
2–3tbsp balsamic vinegar
1tsp green peppercorns in brine or
oil, rinsed and lightly crushed

FRUITS OF THE FOREST SALAD

1 Put the cranberries into a stainless steel pan with 5tbsp water. Cook gently for about 5–10 minutes or until the cranberries pop and are just soft. Remove from the heat, stir in the sugar, and leave until the sugar has dissolved and the mixture has cooled slightly (do not add the sugar at the beginning or it will make the cranberry skins tough).

2 Put the remaining fruit into a serving bowl, add the cooled cranberries and juice, and mix gently together.

3 Add the balsamic vinegar and green peppercorns and mix gently. Cover and chill in the refrigerator for at least 4 hours (or overnight) to allow to juices to develop and the flavours to mellow.

Illustrated on page 241.

CREME CARAMEL

SERVES 6

175g (6oz) granulated sugar
150ml (¼ pint) water
4 eggs
1tsp vanilla extract
30g (1oz) caster sugar
600ml (1 pint) full cream milk
6 small ramekins

1 Combine the sugar and water in a saucepan and heat gently, stirring all the time until all the sugar has dissolved. Bring to a boil, and cook without stirring, until golden. Pour into the ramekins.

2 Whisk the eggs and vanilla extract in a bowl until blended. Heat the milk until just warm, then pour into the egg mixture, whisking well. Strain through a sieve into the ramekins.

3 Put the ramekins in a roasting tin and add enough hot water to come halfway up the sides of the ramekins. Bake in a preheated oven at 160°C (325°F, Gas 3) for about 40 minutes until just set and firm to the touch but not solid. Cool, then chill for 8 hours.

4 Turn out on to individual plates to serve.

Cook's know-how

Vanilla extract gives the best flavour – it is more expensive than vanila essence, but is well worth it.

SORBETS

Light and refreshing, sorbets are the perfect ending to a rich meal. Flavoured with fresh fruits and made from a basic mixture of sugar, water, and egg white, they're also low in fat. Decorate each sorbet with its key ingredient or with an ingredient complementary in flavour.

LIME

SERVES 6–8

250g (8oz) granulated sugar
600ml (1 pint) water
finely grated zest and juice
  of 6 limes
2 egg whites
strips of lime zest to decorate

1 Put the sugar and measured water into a saucepan and heat gently until the sugar dissolves. Bring to a boil and boil for 2 minutes. Remove from the heat, add the lime zest, and leave to cool completely. Stir in the lime juice.

2 Strain the lime syrup into a shallow freezerproof container and freeze for about 2 hours until just mushy. Turn the mixture into a bowl and whisk gently to break down any large crystals.

3 Whisk the egg whites until stiff but not dry, then fold into the lime mixture. Return to the freezer, and freeze until firm. Transfer the sorbet to the refrigerator to soften for about 30 minutes before serving, and top with strips of lime zest.

clockwise from top: *Lime, Raspberry, Pear & Ginger, and Apricot Sorbets.*

PEAR & GINGER

SERVES 6–8

90g (3oz) granulated sugar
300ml (½ pint) water
1tbsp lemon juice
750g (1½lb) pears, peeled
  and cored
1 piece of stem ginger in syrup,
  finely chopped
2 egg whites
strips of stem ginger
  to decorate

1 Put the sugar, measured water, and lemon juice into a saucepan and heat gently until the sugar dissolves. Bring to a boil, add the pears, and poach gently, basting with the sugar syrup from time to time, for 20–25 minutes until the pears are tender. Cool, then purée in a food processor.

2 Add the chopped stem ginger to the pear purée. Pour the pear mixture into a freezerproof container, then follow steps 2 and 3 of lime sorbet (page 246). Decorate with stem ginger before serving.

Illustrated on page 247.

GRANITAS

Italian granitas are similar to sorbets but even easier to make: they are simply flavoured ice crystals.

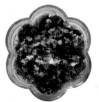

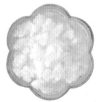

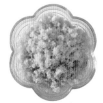

COFFEE
Put 60g (2oz) caster sugar and 4tbsp instant coffee granules into a pan with 750ml (1¼ pints) water and bring to a boil. Simmer for about 5 minutes. Leave to cool, then pour into a freezerproof container. Freeze, stirring occasionally, for 5 hours.

LEMON
Put 200g (7oz) caster sugar into a saucepan, add 500ml (16fl oz) water, and bring to a boil. Simmer for 5 minutes. Leave to cool. Add 2tsp finely grated lemon zest and the juice of 4 lemons to the sugar syrup. Pour into a freezerproof container and freeze, stirring occasionally, for 5 hours..

WATERMELON
Remove and discard the rind and seeds from 1kg (2lb) watermelon. Purée the flesh in a food processor. Pour into a freezerproof container and mix in 30g (1oz) icing sugar and 1½tsp lemon juice. Freeze, stirring occasionally, for 5 hours.

APRICOT

SERVES 6–8

90g (3oz) granulated sugar
300ml (½ pint) water
juice of 1 lemon
750g (1½lb) apricots, halved
   and stoned
2 egg whites

1 Put the sugar, measured water, and lemon juice into a saucepan and heat gently until the sugar has dissolved. Bring to a boil, add the apricots, and simmer for 15 minutes or until very tender. Cool.

2 Peel and slice a few apricots for decoration, and set aside. Press the remainder through a sieve. Mix with the syrup in a freezerproof container, then follow steps 2 and 3 of lime sorbet (page 246). Decorate with the sliced apricots before serving.

Illustrated on page 247.

RASPBERRY

SERVES 6–8

500g (1lb) raspberries
175g (6oz) granulated sugar
600ml (1 pint) water
juice of 1 orange
3 egg whites
raspberries and mint sprigs
   to decorate

1 Purée the raspberries in a food processor. Put the sugar and water into a saucepan and heat until the sugar dissolves. Bring to boil, then boil for 5 minutes.

2 Stir in raspberry purée and orange juice. Pour into a freezerproof container, then follow steps 2 and 3 of lime sorbet (page 246). Decorate with raspberries and mint sprigs before serving.

Illustrated on page 247.

ORANGE PASSION SALAD

SERVES 6

8 thin-skinned oranges
juice of 1 small lime
2 ripe papayas (pawpaws)
3 ripe passion fruit

1 Remove the thin orange skin from 2 of the oranges with a zester and set the strips of zest aside. Peel all the oranges and remove all the skin and pith. Slice into rounds and remove any pips.

2 Put the orange slices into a fairly shallow glass bowl with any juice from the oranges and the lime juice.

3 Halve the papayas lengthwise and scoop out the seeds. Peel the halves, cut crosswise into fairly thick slices, and add to the bowl. Cut the passion fruit in half crosswise, and scoop the juice and pips over the fruit in the bowl. Top the salad with the orange zest, cover, and chill in the refrigerator for at least 2 hours. Stir before serving – there is no need for sugar.

Illustrated on page 241.

FROZEN LEMON FLUMMERY

SERVES 4

150ml (¼ pint) double cream
finely grated zest and juice
  of 1 large lemon
175g (6oz) caster sugar
300ml (½ pint) milk
thinly pared zest of 1 lemon, cut
  into strips, to decorate

1 Whip the cream until it forms soft peaks. Add the lemon zest and juice, caster sugar, and milk, and mix until evenly blended.

2 Pour into a shallow freezerproof container, cover, and freeze for at least 6 hours or until firm.

3 Cut the mixture into chunks, then transfer to a food processor and work until smooth and creamy. Pour into 4 individual freezerproof dishes and freeze for about 8 hours.

4 Blanch the strips of lemon zest in a pan of boiling water for 1 minute only. Drain, rinse, and pat dry.

5 Decorate the flummery with the strips of lemon zest and serve.

Frozen orange flummery

Substitute the finely grated zest and juice of 1 orange for the lemon, and reduce the caster sugar to 125g (4oz). Decorate with blanched strips of orange zest.

INDEX

MARY BERRY

ABOUT THE AUTHOR

Mary Berry is one of the UK's best-known and respected cookery writers, a TV cook and Aga expert, and champion of traditional family cooking. With over 60 books to her name, and over 5 million sales worldwide, in 2004, she was voted Top 3 by *BBC Good Food* for the category "Most Reliable Celebrity Cook Books", alongside Jamie Oliver and Delia Smith.

Throughout the years, Mary Berry has established her style as "family food", with practical healthy recipes containing lots of fresh ingredients. Appearing on numerous TV and Radio programmes, she has shared her culinary secrets with the nation and become a household name, hosting seven cookery series for Thames Television as well as several series for the BBC including *Mary Berry at Home* and *Mary Berry's Ultimate Cakes*, which were filmed at her home in Buckinghamshire.

Mary Berry continues to be a contributor for Radio 4's *Woman's Hour* and the BBC's *Saturday Kitchen*. She also runs hugely popular Aga workshops at her home.

ACKNOWLEDGEMENTS

AUTHOR'S ACKNOWLEDGMENTS FOR *MARY BERRY'S COMPLETE COOKBOOK*

For the first edition, I would like to thank Fiona Oyston for her expertise in writing and testing recipes, and for all her hard work helping me produce the book. I would also like to thank managing editor Gillian Roberts for help in preparing the second edition.

PUBLISHER'S ACKNOWLEDGMENTS FOR *MARY BERRY'S COMPLETE COOKBOOK*

The first (1995) edition of this book was created by Carroll & Brown Ltd for Dorling Kindersley. Thanks to the following people for their help: Editorial consultant, Jeni Wright; Project editor, Vicky Hanson; Editors, Jo-Anne Cox, Stella Vayne, Anne Crane, Sophie Lankenau, and Trish Shine; Cookery consultants, Valerie Cipollone and Anne Hildyard; Art editors, Louise Cameron and Gary Edgar-Hyde; Designers, Alan Watt, Karen Sawyer, and Lucy De Rosa; Photography, David Murray and Jules Selmes, assisted by Nick Allen and Sid Sideris; Production, Wendy Rogers and Amanda Mackie; Food preparation, Eric Treuille, Annie Nichols, Cara Hobday, Sandra Baddeley, and Elaine Ngan, assisted by Maddalena Bastianelli and Sarah Lowman; Additional recipes/Contributors, Marlena Spieler, Sue Ashworth, Louise Pickford, Cara Hobday, Norma MacMillan, and Anne Gains; Nutritional consultant Anne Sheasby.

The second (2003) edition of this book was created by Dorling Kindersley. Thanks to the following people for their help: Editorial contributor, Norma MacMillan; Editorial assistance, Hugh Thompson; DK Picture Library, Claire Bowers and Charlotte Oster; Nutritional consultant, Wendy Doyle; Index, Helen Smith; Loan of props, Villeroy & Boch, Thomas Goode & Co. and Chomett. Thanks also to DK India: Project editor, Dipali Singh; Editor, Kajori Aikat; Project designer, Romi Chakraborty; Designer, Rashmi Battoo; DTP, Narender Kumar, Rajesh Chibber, and Nain Singh Rawat; Managing editor, Ira Pande; Managing art editor, Aparna Sharma.

The publisher would like to thank the following for their kind permission to reproduce their photographs:

(Key: a-above; b-below/bottom; c-centre; l-left; r-right; t-top)

Jacket images: *Front:* **Rob Judges:** tr. *Spine:* **Rob Judges:** t

All other images © Dorling Kindersley
For further information see: www.dkimages.com